The Future
of American Prosperity

THE MACMILLAN COMPANY
NEW YORK · CHICAGO
DALLAS · ATLANTA · SAN FRANCISCO
LONDON · MANILA

THE MACMILLAN COMPANY
OF CANADA, LIMITED
TORONTO

The Future
of American Prosperity

PHILIP WERNETTE

Professor of Business Administration
University of Michigan

THE MACMILLAN COMPANY NEW YORK

First Printing

Preface

The future prosperity of the United States of America is naturally important to Americans. But it is also of considerable importance to the peoples of other nations. Prosperity and economic growth are key forces in international economic relations and in the world's ideological, diplomatic, and military race.

There is considerable disagreement about the outlook for the American economy. Many people foresee growth and prosperity; while some fear depression and wonder whether the economy will grow rapidly enough to maintain maximum employment. In recent years I have lectured from coast to coast before businessmen and bankers on the subject (actually a happy one): "What's Ahead for America?" But whether I am in conservative Boston, dynamic Detroit, busy Minneapolis, or fast-expanding Los Angeles, there never fails to be raised a Voice of gloom, skepticism, and fear. A Voice that accurately states historical facts. A Voice that says, "But, sir, in the late 20's we also had a slogan, 'Prosperity is here to stay,' and yet the 30's followed." A Voice reminding us the AAA, NRA, and WPA tried—and failed— to pull us out of the Great Depression. A Voice that during the full employment of World War II wondered, "Do we have only an unhappy choice of War-and-Prosperity or Peace-and-Depression?" A Voice that loudly supports the balanced budget and therefore "views with alarm" the huge national debt. A Voice that at one and the same time expresses the security based on knowledge of the United States' ability to lead the world in production of atom and hydrogen bombs but doubts our ability to cope with the business cycle.

v

On the lecture platform I can answer the Voice. But outside the lecture halls the Voice is heard; it comes from many Americans who are fearful, doubtful, and gloomy about the future. A book on America's future—as I see it—may enable them to realize why the years ahead will be bright and prosperous. Eventually, perhaps, the Voice will be heard no more.

The central idea of this book is that gloom is completely unwarranted, confidence in the future prosperity of the United States being thoroughly justified. The reasoning in support of this proposition is elaborated and leads to the conclusion that rising prosperity without depression *can* be attained—a prosperity that will carry the average family's income from $5,000 a year in 1954 to $11,000 a year in 1999 (in dollars of the same purchasing power). Nor is this cheerful forecast limited to the United States. Other countries will also experience great economic progress in the decades ahead.

This bright prospect, however, could be changed—by a destructive war or moral and spiritual decay among our people, one possible result from too fast and great an increase of material riches.

The world has entered the Atomic Age—a period of fabulous technological development. Should these scientific discoveries be used for war, the result may be disastrous for mankind. But if they are used for peaceful purposes, the result will be economic progress the like of which the world has never seen!

Discussion of many points in this book has benefited from the suggestions of several experts—Emile Benoit-Smullyan, Seymour E. Harris, A. G. Hart, Marshall Knappen, Richard A. Lester, Paul W. McCracken, Sumner Slichter, and Lyndall F. Urwick. In expressing my warm thanks to them, I do not mean to imply any measure of agreement on their part with any of the analyses or proposals contained in the book.

PHILIP WERNETTE

Contents

TABLES

CHARTS

CHAPTER 1

Problems and Goals

ALL OVER THE UNITED STATES PEOPLE GATHER IN GROUPS FROM TIME to time, and their talk frequently turns to economic problems. Workmen at lunch, executives in conference, farmers at Grange meetings, and women at social gatherings discuss the outlook for employment, wages, prices, and profits. Interest in economic problems is not limited to Americans but is shared by people in all countries.

For centuries men have been concerned with improving their living conditions, but in modern times the general public has become increasingly aware of the significance of national economic policies. As economic society has become more complex, the well-being of every individual and also that of every business have come to be determined less completely by individual efforts and more by great national and international forces, such as inflation and deflation. Moreover, as people have become better educated and as the influence of newspapers, magazines, radio, and television has multiplied, people have come to understand better the importance of these great forces, at least as they affect the person himself.

1

2

It is altogether reasonable that people should be—and are—interested in national economic problems. Moreover, they are concerned and troubled. Some people, disturbed by inflation and the high cost of living, are worrying about the possibility of more inflation in the future. Others, remembering the Great Depression of the 1930's, fear deflation and depression. Some persons, not illogically, are worried about both inflation and deflation. The present basis for American prosperity is thought by some to be precarious. Those taking the longer view wonder whether, in the decades ahead, economic progress will be slow and stagnant, or rapid and vigorous. The importance of future economic strength as this affects ideological struggles and military power looms large in men's minds.

Different groups of people have different special interests, but they all share one in common—the economic health of the nation, which affects everyone; therefore the state of the nation's economy and its future progress and prosperity are important to everyone. The principal groups and their special interests are:

1. Salaried workers and wage-earners realize that their jobs and earnings depend not only on their own efforts but also on the level of general business activity.

2. Independent business men, professional men, farmers, and investors know that their incomes will depend in part on the state of the nation's economy.

3. Parents and grandparents naturally are concerned about the kind of country in which their children and grandchildren will live.

4. Young people—the children and the grandchildren, themselves—ponder the same question. Will America be a land of promise, opportunity, and fulfillment? Or will it be a nation characterized by stagnation, depression, and disappointment?

5. Citizens of our republic—young and old—understand that economic progress provides both a better life and greater national strength. They are interested in the causes of economic progress.

Because of the troubled international situation they are acutely concerned about the future economic strength of their country.

6. People in other countries realize that the ups and downs of American business affect them to some extent, and therefore they are interested in American business conditions.

7. People in other countries also see the importance of economic strength and progress in connection with both ideological struggles and shooting wars. The bigger the country, the more important is the condition of its economy.

These observations, to be sure, do not mean that economic matters are the only things that are important to people or are the only things that concern them. This book, however, is concerned mainly with economic affairs.

HOW CONFIDENT ARE AMERICANS?

What do the American people think about the future? How do the income-earners, the business men, the professional men, the farmers, the investors, the older people, the younger people, and the citizens generally visualize the outlook?

Various pieces of evidence suggest that many Americans are gloomy about the future. One of the most representative indications is a survey made by Dr. George Gallup, the results of which were published on March 15, 1952.* In this survey, representatives of the Gallup organization put the following question to a cross section of American adults: "As you look to the future, do you think life for people generally will get better—or will it get worse?"

The opinions were divided thus:

	Per Cent
Better	42
Worse	34
Same	13
Don't know	11
	100

* American Institute of Public Opinion, release dated March 15, 1952.

The true meaning of these opinions is not entirely clear because one cannot know whether the respondents took the term "people generally" to mean: 1. the people of the United States or 2. the people of the entire world.

It is quite possible, to be sure, that the respondents were unaware of these alternatives. It is also possible that if they mentally separated people in the United States from those elsewhere, they might have believed that it made no difference and that the same answer would apply to the people of all nations of the earth.

If, however, the record of past history is used as a basis for predicting the future, it makes a great deal of difference. The answers are different for different nations.

In past decades and centuries, economic improvement has been substantial in this country and in several other western countries —standards of living have risen to relatively high levels. If these current trends continue, life will be even better in the future for the residents of these nations. On the other hand, there has been little or no improvement in many other countries—their inhabitants are poor. If current trends continue in the future, the life of the people of these nations will improve little or none. A forecast of "about the same" for these countries has a definite historical basis.

THE HISTORICAL RECORD IN THE UNITED STATES

Assuming that the respondents were speaking about the United States, one is impressed by how few said "better." The historical record in this country shows steady improvement in the life of the average man—except in the decade of the 1930's.

The statistics on incomes prior to 1900 are not too reliable. Available figures and knowledge of American home life (past and present), however, suggest that the average American lived much better in 1900 than did the citizens when the republic was young.

The statistical picture since 1900 is more dependable. In 1900 the national income was $16.2 billion. Since the 1900 dollar bought about 3 1/3 times as much as the 1954 dollar (although it could not buy, at any price, personal radio sets, television receivers, airplanes, and many other new products) 1900 income may be changed to $54 billion to convert it into 1954 dollars.

In 1900 the population was slightly more than 76 million, and the average per capita income was about $700. By 1950 national income had risen to $265 billion (in 1954 dollars), population to nearly 152 million, and average per capita income to $1,750. The 1950 per capita income was about 2.5 times that of 1900.

The worker's 1950 income, moreover, was not due to an increase in working hours. On the contrary, the average workweek was 20 per cent shorter than at the start of the century.

Our country's economic development has given the American people the highest income level in our history and also the highest in the world. This statement is not made in any boastful fashion but as a simple statement of fact. Several other countries have comfortable income levels, but the great mass of mankind is very poor. Half of the world's inhabitants have incomes only one tenth (or less) as large as the average American's income. The average American uses seven times as much wool, soap, and tanned leather as does the average person in the rest of the world. A thousand average Americans have 14 times as many radio sets as an average thousand residents of other countries, 20 times as many telephones, 56 times as many passenger automobiles, and 200 times as many television sets.

In view of this record of past growth and present economic standards, is it not interesting that so few Americans (if they meant their responses to apply to this country) expected life in the future to be "better" and so many expected it to be "the same" or "worse"? Is not one justified in asking: Why are so few Americans optimistic, and why do so many have neutral or unfavorable expectations?

THE CASE FOR DOUBT AND FEAR

Some light may be shed on this situation by the history of the period from 1914 to mid-century. This period witnessed many catastrophic occurrences. Two world wars engulfed much of mankind, and a "cold war" and the Korean action troubled the world. The world experienced many inflationary movements of prices—some modest in size, others running to fantastic figures. In the 1930's the United States went through the worst depression in its history, and many other countries also had depressions. Nations went into debt, and some repudiated their debts.

These dismal experiences left a wretched legacy. The threat of war troubles the world. Some people in the United States fear further inflation; others are afraid of deflation and depression; some fear *both* boom and bust. Other worries include the national debt, the cost of the military program, and the long-range outlook for the American economy.

THE OPTIMISTIC THEME OF THIS BOOK

The sorry record of these recent decades does indeed constitute a basis for doubts and fears. The principal theme of this book, however, is that the nation's economic problems not only can be met, but, in addition, if destructive war does not interfere, our future economic progress will be even greater than our past gains. Nor is this favorable view limited to our country. The same proposition is held to apply to many other nations—in varying degrees.

The economic problems of all countries are basically much alike, although their importance varies among the nations. There are three basic economic problems; there is, too, the important matter of *noneconomic* values and problems. The economic problems are these: 1. the problem of poverty, 2. the problem of progress, and 3. the problem of stability.

THE PROBLEM OF POVERTY

The economic state of most of mankind at present can be described in one word—*poverty*. Indeed, very large numbers of people live in a condition of abject poverty that borders on starvation. Figures given in Chapter 4 present the facts in a cold statistical way. In truth, however, for Americans at least, it is probably a fact that these figures hardly convey a convincing picture—the level of poverty in many nations is so much worse than is ordinarily encountered in this country that it probably has to be *seen* in order to be comprehended.

Not all the peoples of the world, of course, live in poverty. Some live in comparative comfort. About a dozen countries—all but four (the United States, Canada, New Zealand, and Australia) located in western Europe—have living standards for the average man that represent comparative comfort. These nations include about one-eighth of the earth's inhabitants.

On the other hand, half of the world's people live at the level of grinding poverty, including most of those in Asia and Africa and a large proportion of the inhabitants of several of the Latin-American republics. The remaining three-eighths of the world's population are poor but live somewhat above the subsistence level.

Why are some nations rich and others poor? How may the standard of living in all lands—rich and poor—be raised? What determines the level of peoples' incomes?

The level of real incomes * depends basically on per capita productivity. This, in turn, is determined by certain definitely identifiable factors, including the quality of the labor force, of management, and of capital goods—to mention only three. If the controlling conditions are unfavorable, a nation will be poor; if

---

* By "real income" is meant the quantity of goods and services that people can buy with their money income. In this book the word "income" means real income unless indicated otherwise.

they are favorable, it will be well off. Similarly, if these factors *improve* in a nation, the standard of living of its people will rise.

THE PROBLEM OF PROGRESS

Many nations have made very little progress in raising their real per capita incomes. China, India, and Egypt are three of the oldest civilizations on earth; apparently their people today live but little better, if any, than did their ancestors hundreds or thousands of years ago. On the other hand, economic progress has been marked in certain other nations, especially in the group of relatively well-to-do countries mentioned above.

The problem of progress is closely related to the problem of poverty. Unfavorable conditions, such as poor health, lack of capital equipment, and absence of enterprise, create poverty. An improvement in conditions leads to a rise of incomes. The rate of economic advance has been high in many countries in modern times.

High though the past rate has been, the future rate of progress may be much faster. If war does not interfere, many of the progressive nations may expect to see their per capita real incomes doubled within the next 50 years. Unless something happens to prevent normal improvement, real per capita incomes in the United States will probably increase by at least 20 per cent per decade, which is equivalent to a gain of 150 per cent in 50 years. Whereas in 1950, per capita income was $1,750, by the year 2000, it will be at least $4,300, barring unfortunate events. During the same period average annual employee earnings will rise from $3,000 to $7,500, and average family income from $4,400 to about $11,000. (All the dollar figures in the preceding sentence have been expressed in 1954 dollars.)

The foregoing figures are in dollars of 1954 purchasing power. Actually, the purchasing power of the 2000-A.D. dollar may be either higher or lower than that of 1954. If so, these income figures should be adjusted upward or downward accordingly. What the figures mean is that real incomes in the United States at the end of the century will be 2.5 times as high as at mid-century. This improvement will occur despite a gradual shortening of the workweek—to perhaps as few as 30 hours per week, with (eventually) the introduction of summer and winter vacations for all workers.

If these figures for the future seem large, compare them with the increase in the first half of this century. The average per capita income, in 1954 dollars, rose from about $700 in 1900 to $1,750 in 1950, a gain of 150 per cent. In view of the immense sums now being spent on research, it is probable that the rate of technological progress will be higher in the future than it was in the past. If so, the rate of economic progress will also be faster.

THE PROBLEM OF STABILITY

Even in the countries that have experienced economic progress, there have been occasional setbacks or periods of depression. These great fluctuations of general business conditions are often called "business cycles." A large proportion of the world, including the United States, experienced an extreme depression in the 1930's. In the United States the depression was very much more severe than any previous one, including even the great ones of the 1870's and the 1890's. One of the desirable conditions for the future is that economic progress should occur with a minimum of cyclical slumps and certainly without any major depressions.

The latter part of this book deals with the problem of stability, with special reference to the United States. Emphasis is placed on the United States for two principal reasons. The first is that this country is such an important and major factor in world affairs that American stability is a prerequisite condition for, and an important contribution to, the stability of many other countries. The second reason is that the stabilization program suggested for the United States would be suitable for some of the other nations.

THE PROBLEM OF NONECONOMIC VALUES

It is not possible to draw a sharp line between economic and noneconomic values. Nevertheless, many values can be recognized as belonging more to one category than to the other.

Man does not live by bread alone. True. And economic values run pretty much in terms of "bread." But economic progress includes facilitating and contributing to the development of noneconomic values.

It is not possible to present a complete list of worthwhile noneconomic values. A partial list, however, might include the following: 1. a sense of satisfaction in one's work; 2. the enjoyment of satisfactory human relations—at work, at home, in the community, and elsewhere; 3. the development in each individual, of good character and a harmonious personality; and 4. progress toward living the good life, as individuals and as a society—characterized by friendliness, courtesy, strength, and other moral and spiritual values.

If all goes well with the world, these broader goals are going to be achieved increasingly for mankind in the decades ahead. In the United States, with luck and wisdom, the economic problem —the problem of making ends meet—is going to be solved for our people within not so many years. This will mean that the national nose can be taken from the economic grindstone. Then both opportunity and incentive will enable us to move far in the direction of the good life. Further attention will be given to this goal in the last chapter of this book.

Nor will economic progress be limited to this country. If a disastrous war does not occur, the half century ahead may well witness more economic improvement throughout the world than has occurred since time began.

SUMMARY

1. The future of American prosperity is important to all Americans and also to the peoples of other lands.

2. Many Americans are doubtful about our country's economic outlook.

3. The theme of this book is that these doubts are unjustified because progress and stability lie ahead, not only for the United States, but also for many other countries—provided that a disastrous war does not occur.

CHAPTER 2

The Nature of Prosperity

THE PROSPERITY OF THE PEOPLE OF ANY NATION CAN BE MEASURED roughly by the average real income per person. Statistically, this figure is usually computed by dividing the total national income of the people of the country by the number of inhabitants. Thus, in 1953 the United States' national income was $305 billion; the population was almost 160 million; the average per capita income was $1,900.

The level of average per capita income is also called the "standard of living" of a country's people.

These three terms, therefore, mean substantially the same thing:

1. Level of prosperity
2. Average per capita real income
3. Standard of living

The "real income" of the people of any nation does not consist of money, but of the stream of goods and services which the people are able to buy with their money incomes. Real income consists of food, clothing, housing, automobiles, and the rest of the necessities and luxuries which people consume.

Real income is related to money income, and is commonly measured and expressed in monetary terms. Thus, when in 1953 the average money income of the people of the United States was $1,900, the average real income was the quantity of goods and services which could be purchased in that year with $1,900.

We may now ask: What determines the level of a nation's real income? The answer is: The magnitude of the nation's *production* of goods and services. Broadly speaking, the people of any nation get to consume the goods and services which they themselves produce. In addition, they also consume some goods that are imported from other countries. But since the imports are paid for by exports, the general principle still holds true.

SUPPLY AND DEMAND

The preceding explanation leads to another question: What determines the size of a nation's output or production?

This depends, in the broadest sense, on supply and demand. As is usually true when these familiar words are used in economic analysis, they stand for a complex of ideas. In this case, "supply" means the size of the stream of goods which a nation is capable of producing. This may be thought of as being a technical or physical concept. Supply means the quantity of goods that the people of a nation can produce when they are fully employed. This supply factor may be referred to as "productive capacity." We shall return later to a discussion of the conditions which make it high or low.

For the present, let us note that productive capacity sets an upper limit to the prosperity of a people. Actual output and income cannot go *above* this amount. They are likely, however, to fall *below* that level if *demand* is inadequate. In this sense, the word "demand" means what is often called "effective demand"— the amount of money which people are willing and able to pay for goods and services.

The manner in which demand affects national production is this: Goods will be produced only if they are likely to be sold. Hence, demand also places an upper limit on production.

To repeat, then: *Supply* sets an upper limit on production because it determines the size of *potential* output. *Demand* determines *actual* output, within the limit of the existing potential output.

Demand determines the level of "business cycle prosperity," as distinguished from the level of productive capacity. The demand factor is especially important in the United States, since, for reasons that will be discussed later, demand can vary greatly in this country.

THE CONDITIONS OF ECONOMIC PROGRESS

The levels of national production and income are determined, then, by supply and demand. In a depression, inadequacy of demand causes actual production to fall below existing potential output. In a period of cyclical prosperity, actual production rises to the level of capacity output.

We are concerned, however, not merely with national and per capita incomes as they now are, but also with the problem of raising them in future decades. The problem of increasing them involves expanding both the supply and the demand factors.

In most countries of the world, the problem of supply—productive capacity—is more important than the problem of cyclical prosperity.

In the United States, both problems are important. The level of basic prosperity is already high, but we would like to see it higher. Furthermore, we do not want to see actual prosperity fall much (if at all) below potential prosperity in future years. In other words, we do not want to witness another depression.

The interaction of supply and demand factors as well as their effects on prosperity are illustrated in Table 1 and Chart 1, which show the average per capita real income of the United States

TABLE 1. REAL PER CAPITA INCOME IN THE UNITED STATES, 1922-1950

Year	In Current Dollars (A)	Index of Consumer Prices (1935–39 = 100) (B)	Index Divided By 1,691 (C)	In 1949 Dollars $\frac{(A)}{(C)}$
1922	$ 550	119.7	0.708	$ 777
1923	626	121.9	.721	868
1924	614	122.2	.723	849
1925	646	125.4	.742	871
1926	655	126.4	.747	877
1927	642	124.0	.733	876
1928	666	122.6	.724	920
1929	717	122.5	.724	990
1930	610	119.4	.706	864
1931	475	108.7	.643	739
1932	326	97.6	.577	565
1933	315	92.4	.546	577
1934	384	95.7	.566	678
1935	445	98.1	.580	767
1936	505	99.1	.587	860
1937	571	102.7	.607	941
1938	520	100.8	.596	872
1939	554	99.4	.588	942
1940	616	100.2	.593	1,039
1941	780	105.2	.622	1,254
1942	1,018	116.5	.689	1,478
1943	1,243	123.6	.731	1,700
1944	1,331	125.5	.742	1,794
1945	1,309	128.4	.759	1,725
1946	1,277	139.3	.824	1,550
1947	1,380	159.2	.941	1,467
1948	1,525	171.2	1.012	1,507
1949	1,449	169.1	1.000	1,449
1950	1,585	171.9	1.017	1,559

Sources: For per capita income figures, see Table 15, pp. 131–132. For index of consumer prices, see "Index of Consumer Prices," *Federal Reserve Bulletin*, July 1951, p. 851.

Note: The adjusted figures in the last column for the years 1942–1948, inclusive, are misleading because price control kept prices artificially low.

from 1922 to 1950. The incomes are expressed in terms of 1949 dollars—that is, in prices equal to 1949 prices.

In Chart 1 the figures for 1942 to 1947 have been omitted in computing the long-time trend. During these years price controls and rationing restrained a rise in the price level. The existence of a temporary legal ceiling on prices makes the calculated real income figures deceptively high. If prices had been allowed to rise without restraint, the wartime *real* income figures would have risen much less than they did. Furthermore, a large portion of wartime incomes was actually unspendable, since goods simply were not available. The consequence was an abnormally high level of saving.

The steady increase of the supply factor—potential per capita production—is shown by the dotted line. The tremendous drop

CHART 1. REAL PER CAPITA INCOME IN THE
UNITED STATES, 1922–1950

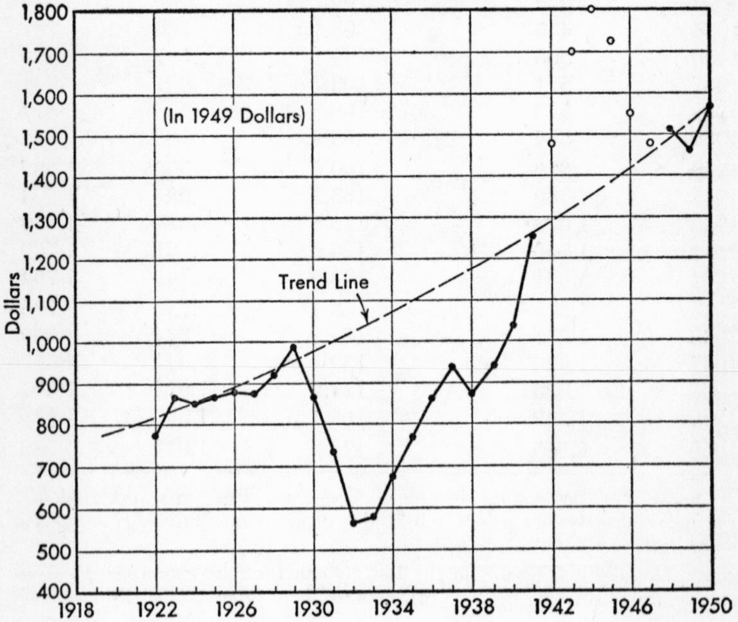

in actual per capita income below potential income during the thirties is indicated clearly.

This drop was caused by a decline in the demand factor. How can we be sure that it was caused by a slump in demand rather than by a drop in productive capacity? The facts of employment and unemployment make it clear that inability to find work rather than a drop in man-hour output was the explanation.

In 1933, for example, national production was about 65 per cent of the potential figure. About 75 per cent of the work force was employed, and the average workweek (many were employed only part-time) was about 85 per cent of normal. The product of these last two figures ($0.75 \times 0.85 = 0.64$) indicates 64 per cent of normal employment; this comes very close to the computed deficiency.

That the supply factor was expanding during the depression period is shown by the rise in the indexes of output per man-hour. Table 2 shows the trend during the depression.

TABLE 2. OUTPUT PER MAN-HOUR IN THE
UNITED STATES, 1929–1939
(1939 = 100)

Year	All Manu-facturing	Railroad Trans-portation	Mining	Electric Light and Power
1929	78.1	75.1	69.9	54.1
1930	80.0	75.1	72.9	50.1
1931	83.5	75.6	77.2	51.9
1932	77.8	73.7	77.6	58.3
1933	81.9	83.0	78.8	68.1
1934	85.9	83.7	81.4	77.4
1935	90.8	87.6	84.9	82.5
1936	91.0	93.5	86.6	87.8
1937	90.0	95.2	88.0	89.6
1938	91.6	94.7	90.1	89.0
1939	100.0	100.0	100.0	100.0

SOURCE: U.S. Bureau of the Census, *Historical Statistics of the United States* (Washington: U.S. Government Printing Office, 1949), p. 71.

THE LONG-RANGE FUTURE
OF THE AMERICAN ECONOMY

Chart 1 also indicates the upward trend in American prosperity which has prevailed when both supply and demand factors have been favorable. If these factors remain favorable—and subsequent analysis will be directed to the problem of how to keep them favorable—economic progress in this country may be expected to continue into the indefinite future.

A few years ago some analysts were forecasting something quite different. They asserted that ours had become a "mature economy," and they propounded the "stagnation thesis." If by "mature" they had meant that we were no longer a primitive society, that we were in some sense or other grown-up, they would have been right. But that is not what they meant. What they really meant was that we were approaching senility, that our country had stopped growing, that population growth and economic advance were going to level out and perhaps start on the downgrade. A natural enough mistake, it resulted from confusing the worst depression in our history—that of the 1930's—with a reversal of the long-time growth trends of the United States. Those analysts were wrong, and subsequent events have proved that they were wrong.

Let's take a look ahead, then, at the future growth of our country.

If all goes well (and the meaning of that qualification will be discussed later on), here are some estimates of the future growth of the United States.

POPULATION GROWTH

The recent, rapid growth of the population, caused by a large increase in the number of births, has confounded many population forecasts that were made a few years back. Those forecasts suggested a gradually slower increase in the population, which was expected to reach a peak of perhaps 165,000,000 in the 1980's and then decrease. The few earlier forecasts that disagreed with this view, projecting large and continuing increases, were criticized.

Actually, births rose from 2,307,000 in 1933 (the smallest number since 1910 when records became satisfactory) to 3,881,000 in 1952. The birth rate per thousand of the population increased from 18.4 in 1933 (probably the lowest in the nation's history) to 24.9 in 1952. The factors responsible for the reversal of the earlier trend seem to be: 1. a shift of parental sentiment in favor of having more children and 2. higher incomes.

If this new trend continues, population growth will continue to be substantial. As a basis for estimates, we may use the figures for recent decades. From 1920 to 1930 the population rose from 106.5 million to 123.1 million (15.6 per cent); from 1930 to 1940 it increased to 132.0 million (a gain of 7.2 per cent); and by 1950 it had jumped to 151.7 million (an increase of 14.9 per cent). The following table presents a projection of future population growth in the United States, assuming a decennial increase of 15 per cent.

TABLE 3.   POPULATION PROJECTION THROUGH
THE YEAR 2000

Year		Population
Actual	Projected	(*Millions*)
1900		76.1
1950		151.7
	1960	174
	1970	200
	1980	230
	1990	264
	2000	304

THE GROWTH OF INCOMES

It might be supposed that such a substantial population growth would have the "Malthusian" effect of reducing our living standards. Not so, however. Our living standards will continue to rise, concurrently with a population increase, as the two have risen simultaneously in the past.

Average per capita real incomes may be expected to rise as output per man-hour increases. How rapidly will this output increase? It has increased at about 2 per cent per year in recent decades. Since many times as much research is being carried on as the amount done in earlier decades, an estimate of a future annual gain at the same rate—2 per cent—is conservative. Since the workweek will also be reduced gradually, the decennial increase in annual output per worker may be taken to be slightly less than 2 per cent compounded annually for ten years, or about 20 per cent. Average per capita real incomes will, therefore, rise 20 per cent per decade, provided that the work force remains in the same relationship, proportionately, to the total population.

Table 4 brings together the population projections and the per capita income estimates and presents a projection for the national income. If the decennial rate of increase in output per man-hour should turn out to be greater than 20 per cent (as it easily may), the figures for per capita income and national income would have to be raised correspondingly.

It must be emphasized that this expansion will not come about automatically. It will occur if private enterprise is increasingly effective and if government policies are sound. If these conditions are fulfilled, productive capacity will continue to rise, and cyclical prosperity will ensure that actual national income is at, or close to, potential national income. Suggestions of ways of encouraging prosperity and expansion are presented in later chapters.

This picture of future growth has a large dark cloud—the possi-

TABLE 4.   PROJECTIONS FOR THE UNITED STATES OF
FUTURE POPULATION, PER CAPITA INCOME,
AND NATIONAL INCOME

Year		Population	Average per Capita Income	National Income
Actual	Projected	(Millions)	(1954 dollars)	(Billions of 1954 dollars)
1900[a]		76.1	$ 700	$ 54
1950[a]		151.7	1,750	264
	1960	174	2,100	365
	1970	200	2,500	500
	1980	230	3,000	690
	1990	264	3,600	950
	2000	304	4,300	1,300

[a] Actual figures for 1900 and 1950 have been converted into 1954 dollars.

bility of war. A disastrous war might cut down the population,
productive capacity, and national income. The international situation is discussed in Chapters 15 and 16.

SUMMARY

1. Two sets of factors control prosperity: *supply*, which depends
on productive capacity and *demand*, which determines the level
of cyclical prosperity.

2. Productive capacity has grown fairly steadily in the United
States, but actual production declined and remained low in the
1930's because of the inadequacy of demand.

3. Population, output per man-hour, and total national income
will grow substantially in future decades, if all goes well.

CHAPTER 3

Productive Capacity—Its Nature and Causes

THE LEVEL OF PRODUCTIVE CAPACITY DEPENDS ON THE FOLLOWING basic factors:

1. The productive efficiency of the working population
2. The quality and quantity (per capita) of natural resources—land, timber, minerals, rainfall, and climate
3. The quality and quantity (per capita) of business management
4. The quality and quantity (per capita) of capital goods—factories, business buildings, machinery, engines, and equipment
5. The quality and quantity (per capita) of risk-taking enterprise
6. The government

If these elements are favorable, output per man-hour will be high; if they are unfavorable, it will be low.

Having noted the factors that control the level of productive capacity, we may next inquire into the circumstances which in turn cause them to be favorable or unfavorable.

THE PRODUCTIVE EFFICIENCY OF THE
WORKING POPULATION

The productive efficiency of the working population depends on several conditions. Let us list some of the principal conditions and examine the conditions that encourage them.

1. *Education.* From the simple skills—reading, writing, and arithmetic—to the professional skills of the engineer, the physician, and the lawyer, education contributes to production. In other important but less obvious ways education contributes—by stimulating imagination, curiosity, and ambition. Public funds spent on education constitute an investment in the future standard of living.

2. *Industriousness.* Output is influenced by how hard people work. The more diligently they work, the greater is their production. If they are not industrious, their output is reduced. The level of industriousness of people is influenced by inheritance, climate, health, attitudes, opportunities, customs, and mores.

3. *Status of labor-management relations.* Poor labor-management relations result in an indifferent attitude on the part of employees and may give rise to strikes and lost production. Conversely, good labor-management relations are conducive to diligent work and high output.

4. *Incentives.* The payment of wages on the basis of productive merit encourages workers to increase their output. Other psychological considerations, especially those associated with good personnel practices, are important, also.

5. *Restriction of output.* Any attitudes or policies that artificially hold down the amount of output which workers are permitted to produce decrease per capita production.

6. *Effective use of the work force.* Effective use of a nation's workers depends in part on each man's being in the occupation and in the place where he can be the most productive. This is a matter of social, geographical, and industrial mobility.

The first of these depends greatly on the absence of social stratification. Social stratification denies the children of poor parents the opportunity to rise to their potential levels. It does so by denying them an opportunity for higher education and perhaps by discouraging or even prohibiting them from rising above their parents' class. Thus in a stratified society, the brilliant son of poor parents who might become a great scientist, helping mightily to raise the nation's output, spends his life as a day laborer. The loss is the nation's, as well as the individual's.

Effective use of the work force is also aided by a good system of employment offices. By making information available about job opportunities, both local and in other communities, the office staffs reduce unemployment and aid workers in moving to better, more productive positions. Conversely, if such information is lacking, workers may remain unemployed, or be employed in less productive work than they are capable of doing.

7. *Sobriety.* Without going into all aspects of the matter of consumption of alcoholic beverages, attention may be drawn to two matters. The first is that expenditure on these commodities may absorb money that could be better spent on other things, for example, food for the family's children. The second is that alcoholism may reduce the working efficiency of a bread-winner. In some nations, excessive drinking is reported to be a national economic problem.

8. *Honesty.* Business operations are handicapped by dishonesty. One form is stealing from employers by employees. In areas where this occurs, therefore, it is reported that no business can have more employees than can be watched personally by the owner. It follows that large-scale (or even medium-scale) businesses cannot be established in such places—thereby preventing the gains from larger business operations. A moment's thought will indicate that a country unable to develop large stores, factories, and other productive enterprises, is handicapped in the economic struggle. Even in such a country's small businesses, a

sizable part of the owner's efforts must go into his police activities —effort that could be used in better ways.

Nor are the adverse effects of dishonesty limited to the employer-employee relationship. Dishonesty is an inconvenience also to householders, buyers, consumers, travelers, motorists, and many other groups.

These difficulties are reduced in proportion to the prevalence of honesty among a people. Economic activity is encouraged in various ways if people customarily are honest.

All this may seem to be only an unnecessary and irrelevant excursion into prosaic copybook maxims. It will not seem so, however, to persons who have had firsthand contact with conditions of dishonesty. To such persons, the observation that "Honesty is the best policy" may be admittedly trite but true.

9. *Health.* Poor health is a double drain on a nation. On the one hand, he who is ill works less, and on the other hand, needs care. Good health (which requires good food), conversely, represents a double gain. In many parts of the world malnutrition and disease are widespread. A sick man cannot work effectively any more than a sick horse can. Typhoid, yaws, malaria, and other diseases make millions of humans miserable and unproductive.

NATURAL RESOURCES

Natural resources include the useful things which nature has given to a nation—land, climate, minerals, water, and timber being the most important.

Natural resources are an important factor in determining a nation's per capita income, but their importance is easily and often exaggerated. One of the commonest explanations, for instance, of the wealth of the United States is its rich natural resources. It is true that this country was endowed with magnificent natural resources. The experts say, however, that there are four other countries whose natural resources are at least equal to ours. They are

Canada, Brazil, China, and Russia. Canada is a rich country, but the others are poor.

The explanation of this paradox is simple enough—most natural resources have to be *developed* in order to be useful. Land often has to be cleared before it can be cultivated. Minerals must be located, extracted, and refined. Timber must be felled and, in many cases, transported over considerable distances. Utilization of water power requires capital investment.

In Brazil, China, and the U.S.S.R. the natural resources have not been developed as extensively as in the United States. Why not? Essentially because the other productive factors are not very effective. The development of natural resources requires enterprise, capital, exploration, management, hard work—in other words, the activities of the *human* resources of a nation. The importance of the human resources is further emphasized by noting the high income level of countries like Denmark, Norway, and Switzerland—nations which are provided with relatively few natural resources.

Natural resources assume greater significance in terms of the ratio of the population to the resources. A large, populous country may have more natural resources than does a small country. Suppose, for example, that the large country has *twice* the amount of natural resources. But if it has *four* times the population, the smaller country is better off in terms of the *per capita* quantity of natural resources. This same proposition applies to three of the other influential elements listed at the beginning of this chapter— capital, management, and enterprise.

The ratio between any (or all) of these factors, on the one hand, and population, on the other, can be altered by changing either the factor(s) or the population.

THE POPULATION QUESTION

The larger the population of a country, the more mouths there are to be fed and the more pairs of hands to work. Will twice as many hands, however, produce twice as much food? The answer that is right most of the time is "No." This is because of the tendency toward diminishing returns.

The general rule is this: At any moment and with given quantities of the other productive factors, an increase in the number of workers will cause total output to increase, but (after a point) the additional output resulting from each additional worker will decrease. In other words, the *marginal product* of each added worker declines.

This principle is often misunderstood by virtue of its being misstated. The rule does *not* say that if, *over a period of years,* the number of workers increases the marginal product will decline. This proposition, to be sure, *might* be true, if the combination of the other productive factors were unchanged. If, however, during these years the amounts of capital, management, and enterprise are also increased by properly proportioned increments, the marginal product may *rise* during the time that the number of workers grows. But the fact remains that by the end of the period the marginal product might have been still higher if the number of workers had not increased at all, or had not increased so much.

The tendency to diminishing returns is probably more significant in agriculture than in manufacturing. It is especially important, therefore, in the underdeveloped countries, in which agriculture is the principal form of production.

Further consideration will be given in the next chapter to the population question, with special reference to the poorer countries. For the present, let it suffice to recognize that the ratio of population to the other productive factors is an important element affecting per capita productivity.

BUSINESS MANAGEMENT

Economic activity does not "run itself." Or at least when it does, it is not well run. Efficient operation of business activity requires organization and administration. These are the roles of business management. The more skilled the managers and the more numerous the skilled managers, the more efficient is the economic system.

What are the circumstances, then, that conduce to a plentiful supply of good business management?

1. *Opportunity for training.* This may be provided either in the educational system or within industry itself.

2. *Incentives.* Good pay for good work, pride in success (and its opposite—fear of failure), ambition, the desire to be respected, and other motivations constitute the incentives to do a good management job.

3. *Other influences.* Some of the comments made above in connection with the effectiveness of the working population apply also to managers. Some of these favorable conditions are: education, industriousness, and industrial mobility.

CAPITAL GOODS

The operator of a huge *power shovel* can move more dirt than can a worker with a spade. Even counting the man-hours that went into *making* the power shovel (which should be counted), the amount of dirt moved per man-hour is greater. The operator has a machine to help him—moreover, it is a *power-driven machine.*

This is perhaps the most obvious of all the factors that contribute to productive capacity. Workers who have the assistance of power-driven machinery—in the factory or on the farm—can produce more than workers who have only hand tools and human power.

What are the circumstances that help to increase the quality and quantity of such capital goods?

1. *Saving.* People may save money to provide for a rainy day or for some similar purpose, or for the explicit purpose of providing funds for capital investment. Either way, however, saving is

necessary in order to permit the accumulation of capital. More-over, the maintenance of capital requires that there should not be *dis-saving*, i.e., an excess of consumption over income.

2. *Investing*. Saving by itself, however, creates no capital goods. The creation of capital goods requires investing—putting money into capital goods. Indeed, the *total* amount of investing actually determines the *total* amount of saving.

3. *Incentives*. People may *save* with no expectation of earning a return, but they rarely *invest* their money except in response to an expectation of making a profit. Adequate profits, therefore, conduce to the expanding of the nation's capital equipment. If the adequacy of profits is genuinely threatened—say, by improper taxation or by too high a wage scale—the effect is adverse to investment and capital formation.

4. *Invention*. There will be no power shovels, tractors, or other machines unless some one invents and develops them. Research and technical training contribute to capital development and make new machines available for use in production.

5. *Attitude of labor*. Many new machines and new methods may be described as (a) "labor-saving" or as (b) "output-increasing." A power shovel may be thought of as saving the labor of many men or as increasing the production of the men who make and use it.

Not infrequently, laborers (either organized or unorganized) have resisted the introduction of new machinery and new production methods, fearing that they would lose their jobs. In some cases the fear has been justified. But even in those cases, the introduction of output-increasing methods has created new jobs and raised the general standard of living.

6. *Knowledge*. Knowledge, including what is currently referred to as "know-how," is one of a nation's greatest assets. It may, therefore, be listed as a part of its capital. Knowledge increases productivity—by increasing the effectiveness of workers, of management, of capital suppliers, of enterprisers, and of gov-

ernment officers. Knowledge, therefore, might be listed separately under each of these factors. Doing so would hardly overstress its importance—that is scarcely possible.

ENTERPRISE

Enterprise is closely related to management and to capital investment, but it is not quite the same as either. It means undertaking new things. The new things may be new consumer products —the automobile, radios, or television. Or they may be new methods of making things—the use of new sources of power, of new machinery, or of new production methods. Or they may be new businesses, in already-established lines, as illustrated by the multiplication of self-service laundries, bowling alleys, and motels.

The vigor of enterprise depends on several factors.

1. Incentives. What has been said above about the importance of incentives to workers, managers, and investors applies also to enterprise. Profits and earnings are incentives to enterprise.

2. Spirit of the people. The very spirit of a community, a state, or a nation may be vigorous and enterprising; on the other hand, it may be somnolent, lethargic, or self-satisfied. Americans seem to be "born inventors." They develop new things and promote them energetically. Vigorous enterprise leads to new products, increased output, and lower costs.

3. Competition. Active competition is a spur to enterprise and progress; its absence is conducive to lethargy and a static economy.

4. Governmental policies. These may help or hinder enterprise and investment. Excessive regulation, high taxes, or improper governmental competition (or even the threat thereof) can weaken enterprise.

So important, indeed, is the matter of governmental policies that we shall give special attention to this area of analysis.

THE GOVERNMENT AND PRIVATE ENTERPRISE

The foregoing explanations of the conditions of productive capacity suggest that the important factors are largely determined by individual initiative and personal responsibility. These are vital characteristics of the private enterprise system.

What, however, is the role of the government in influencing the level of prosperity? The government (national, state, or local, as appropriate) can either aid or injure prosperity, depending on whether its policies, actions, or inactions are favorable or are unfavorable.

Certain basic governmental activities are clearly helpful in promoting prosperity. These include:

1. Protection of persons from violence
2. Protection of rights in property
3. Enforcement of contracts
4. Prevention of fraud
5. Protection of the public safety, health, and morals
6. Provision of highways and a postal system
7. Provision of free education
8. Creation and operation of a proper monetary system
9. Protection from foreign enemies

These activities cost money, which is raised by taxation. Taxation is an economic burden, but it may be justified. The justification for taxation depends on the ways in which the tax money is spent. If the gains from public expenditure outweigh the losses from taxation, the operation is justified—provided that the distribution of the gains among the people and the distribution of the taxation are equitable.

OTHER GOVERNMENTAL ACTIVITIES

Governmental units in the United States have gone far beyond the functions listed above. Their additional activities include the following:

Governmental units *assist* economic activity—by research, publications, subsidies, and conservation of natural resources.

Governmental units *regulate* many businesses and business activities—railroads, public utilities, antitrust policies, pricing policies, food preparation, and labor relations.

Governmental units *influence* economic activity by welfare programs, unemployment compensation, workmen's compensation, and in other ways.

Governmental units *operate* some businesses—credit agencies, the post offices, hydroelectric power plants, and municipal water plants.

Many of these governmental activities are controversial. It is not possible in a book of this size to deal with each on its merits. Suffice it to say, therefore, that in a private enterprise system the burden of proof for these activities rests upon their advocates. Proof may be forthcoming, but additions to these activities should be scrutinized carefully, lest their proliferation slowly and subtly weaken the private enterprise system.

THE GOVERNMENT AND THE BUSINESS CYCLE

The latter part of this book is concerned with the problem of preventing future depressions—of keeping *actual* prosperity close to the level of expanding *potential* prosperity in the future. Analysis leads to the conclusion that an essential part of the prosperity program is a functional fiscal-monetary system. The operation of this system cannot be a function of private enterprise; it can be a function only of the federal government.

It may be said at this point that the proposed fiscal-monetary system does not involve government regulation or regimentation. The aim of the system is to permit the private enterprise system to operate at full speed, because this system ensures a growing, adequate demand for goods. The role of the government is to provide the conditions essential to cyclical prosperity and expansion, so that private enterprise can operate freely and profitably and the people can enjoy full employment and stable, rising incomes.

SUMMARY

1. The level of per capita production (which provides per capita real income) depends on several factors. These include: the characteristics of the workers; the per capita quality of developed natural resources, business management, capital goods, and enterprise; and wise governmental policies.

2. We have looked at some of the conditions that explain and control these factors. These underlying conditions will be examined in greater detail in the next chapters.

CHAPTER 4

The Problem of World Prosperity

MOST OF THE PEOPLE OF THE WORLD LIVE IN POVERTY. THIS IS NOT a new condition; it has prevailed throughout human history. The peoples of many nations, however, have raised their respective standards of living greatly in the past two centuries—notably the United States, Great Britain, Canada, New Zealand, Australia, Japan, certain countries in Europe, and Latin America. In the remaining countries the average standard of living is low, and in some, notably China and India, it borders on mere existence.

It is probably impossible to calculate the per capita incomes of different countries and present them in some common currency or in some other comparable fashion *with a high degree of accuracy.* There are too many difficulties. Nevertheless, attempts have been made to make such estimates. One of the most recent and most comprehensive of such efforts was that of the Statistical Office of the United Nations, whose report, *National and Per Capita Incomes of Seventy Countries in 1949 Expressed in United States Dollars,* was published in October, 1950. The per capita figures given in that report are presented in Table 5.

The United Nations statisticians explain quite frankly that the

TABLE 5. NATIONAL INCOME, POPULATION, AND PER CAPITA INCOMES IN 70 COUNTRIES IN 1949

Country	National Income (Millions of U.S. dollars)	Population (Thousands)	Per Capita Income (U.S. dollars)
Afghanistan	600	12,000 [a]	50
Argentina	5,722	16,555	346
Australia [b]	5,374	7,912	679
Austria	1,516	7,000	216
Belgium	5,015	8,614	582
Bolivia	221	3,990 [a]	55
Brazil	5,530	49,340	112
Burma [b]	612	17,180	36
Canada	11,797	13,549	870
Ceylon	487	7,297	67
Chile	1,070	5,709	188
China	12,384	463,493 [a]	27
Colombia	1,456	11,015	132
Costa Rica	105	837	125
Cuba	1,550	5,199	296
Czechoslovakia	4,625	12,463	371
Denmark	2,908	4,230	689
Dominican Republic	170	2,277	75
Ecuador	134	3,378 [a]	40
Egypt	1,989	20,045	100
El Salvador	197	2,150	92
Ethiopia	570	15,000 [a]	38
Finland	1,399	4,015	348
France	19,857	41,180	482
Germany [c]	15,300	47,585	320
Greece	1,008	7,852	128
Guatemala	293	3,784	77
Haiti	150	3,750 [a]	40
Honduras	110	1,326	83
Hungary	2,315	9,165	269

Note: See footnotes at end of table, p. 37.

TABLE 5. (Cont.)

Country	National Income (Millions of U.S. dollars)	Population (Thousands)	Per Capita Income (U.S. dollars)
Iceland	66	139	476
India [b]	19,572	346,000	57
Indonesia	2,000	79,260 [a]	25
Iran	1,450	17,073 [a]	85
Iraq	424	4,990	85
Ireland	1,260	2,991	420
Israel	395	1,016	389
Italy	10,800	45,996	235
Japan	8,260	82,636	100
Korea [d]	700	20,189	35
Lebanon	155	1,240	125
Liberia	62	1,648 [a]	38
Luxembourg	162	295	553
Mexico	2,960	24,448	121
Netherlands	5,000	9,956	502
New Zealand [e]	1,610	1,881	856
Nicaragua	105	1,184	89
Norway	1,898	3,233	587
Pakistan	3,760	73,855 [a]	51
Panama	140	764	183
Paraguay	109	1,304 [a]	84
Peru	820	8,240	100
Philippines	850	19,356	44
Poland	7,344	24,500	300
Portugal	2,150	8,491	250
Saudi Arabia	240	6,000 [a]	40
Southern Rhodesia	204	2,022 [a]	101
Sweden	5,426	6,956	780
Switzerland	3,940	4,640	849
Syria	340	3,407 [a]	100

Note: See footnotes at end of table, p. 37.

TABLE 5. (*Cont.*)

Country	National Income (*Millions of U.S. dollars*)	Population (*Thousands*)	Per Capita Income (*U.S. dollars*)
Thailand	650	17,987	36
Turkey	2,452	19,623	125
Union of South Africa [b]	3,200	12,112	264
U.S.S.R.	59,500	193,000 [a]	308
United Kingdom	38,922	50,363	773
United States	216,831	149,215	1,453
Uruguay	779	2,353	331
Venezuela	1,478	4,595	322
Yemen	280	7,000 [a]	40
Yugoslavia	2,343	16,040	146
Totals	$513,101	2,083,888	
Average			$246

[a] Rough estimate of population. [b] 1948–1949. [c] Western Zone.
[d] South Korea. [e] 1949–1950.

SOURCE: Statistical Office of the United Nations, *National and Per Capita Incomes of Seventy Countries in 1949, Expressed in United States Dollars* (New York: 1950), pp. 14–16.

figures for some countries are much more reliable than those for others and that the problem of translating income figures from other currencies into U.S. dollars is a difficult one. The income figures, particularly for the underdeveloped countries, are sub-ject to a wide margin of possible error.

These United Nations figures for per capita incomes may be compared with other estimates of per capita incomes and also with Dr. Bennett's * estimates of consumption levels. In Table 6 comparative figures are presented in terms of per capita income in the United States.

* Dr. M. K. Bennett, "International Disparities in Consumption Levels," *American Economic Review,* September 1951, p. 648.

TABLE 6. INDICATORS OF RELATIVE REAL PER CAPITA INCOMES IN 20 COUNTRIES

(United States = 100)

COUNTRY	INCOME RELATIVES			CONSUMPTION RELATIVES	POPU- LATION
	1949	1939	1925–1934	1934–1938	1949 *(Millions)*
	(col. A)	(col. B)	(col. C)	(col. D)	(col. E)
United States	100	100	100	100	149
Canada	60	70	80	84	14
United Kingdom	58[a]	84	76	77	50
Australia	47	73	67	81	8
France	33[a]	51	48	57	41
Czechoslovakia	25[a]	24		45	12
Argentina	24	39	65	50	17
Germany	22[a, b]	94	47	61	48[b]
U.S.S.R.	21[a]	28 (21)	21 (14)	31 (21)	193
Cuba	20	18		37	5
Italy	16[a]	25	20	38	46
Yugoslavia	10[a]	17		24	16
Brazil	8	8 (6)		29 (19)	49
Mexico	8	11		27	24
Japan	7[a]	17	17	38	83
Egypt	7	15 (11)		18 (12)	20
India	3.9	6.1 (4.7)[c]	9 (6)[c]	17 (11)	346
Philippines	3.2	5.8 (4.3)		22 (15)	19
China	1.9	5.2 (3.9)	4.4 (2.9)	14 (9)	463
Indonesia	1.7	4.0 (3.0)		12 (8)	79

[a] Countries whose 1949 income levels were lowered by World War II.
[b] Western Zone.
[c] Then included Pakistan (1949 population, 74 million).

SOURCES: By column letter.

A and E. Statistical Office of the United Nations, *op. cit.*

B. "National Advisory Council on International Monetary and Financial Problems," reported in U.S. Department of State publication, *Point Four* (Washington: U.S. Government Printing Office, 1950), pp. 113, 114.

C. Calculated from figures presented by Colin Clark in Chapter II, *The Conditions of Economic Progress* (1st ed., London: Macmillan & Co., Ltd., 1940) and from those used in the diagram on page 43 of his *The Economics of 1960* (London: Macmillan & Co., Ltd., 1942).

D. Dr. M. K. Bennett, "International Disparities in Consumption Levels," *American Economic Review*, September 1951, p. 648.

Note: Figures within parentheses are revised relatives.

A COMPARISON OF FIGURES

Table 6 presents the figures for all the countries for which at least three of the series were available. The nations listed include all the most populous countries—the twelve with 1949 populations of more than 25 million, except Pakistan. In the earlier years, that nation was part of India. The United Nations figure for Pakistan's 1949 per capita income was $57, as against $51 for India.

The 20 countries included in the table had a total 1949 population of 1,682 million, or about 70 per cent of the estimated world population of 2,400 million.

It is not to be expected that the relative figures for any one country should be exactly the same in the several columns. They differ for several reasons. They relate to different periods of time, and substantial changes occurred during these years. For example, per capita consumption in the United States was about one-third higher in 1949 than in 1939 and about one-half greater in 1949 than in the earlier periods, 1925–34 and 1934–38. If per capita consumption in another country, on the other hand, was the same in 1949 as it had been in the earlier periods, its figure, relative to the United States as 100, would in 1949 be only three-fourths of what it had been in 1939 and only two-thirds of what it had been from 1925–34 and 1934–38. Computations, reflecting this (unchanged) condition have been made for the countries for which this was judged by the author to be true. *The revised relatives are given in parentheses.*

The other important change resulted from the destruction and dislocation of World War II, which caused the 1949 figures for several countries to be (temporarily) abnormally *low*. The countries which were judged by the author to be affected thus have been followed by the super letter *a*.

When allowance is made for this factor, and the previously mentioned adjustments are made, the figures for each country in the first four columns are somewhat similar. There are, however, some disparities, and there is a notable difference between figures in Column *D* and comparable items in the first three columns.

It will be noted that the countries stand in roughly the same rank order in columns *A* to *D*. There are a few arresting differences, however. In Column *A*, Canada, Australia, and Argentina are low, compared with the other columns. In Column *B*, Germany is high and Czechoslovakia low. In Column *C*, Argentina is high. In each of these cases, the disparity is suspicious.

There is one larger difference—between the consumption relatives in Column *D* and the per capita income figures in Columns *A*, *B*, and *C*. The farther down the columns one looks, the greater this difference is seen to be. Column *D*, in short, suggests that the poor countries are not as much poorer than the rich countries as do the other columns.

This is to be expected. As Dr. Bennett * points out, his figures are not meant to be indicators of per capita incomes, and they include certain factors that are not part of, or the same thing as, per capita income—such as a warm or cold climate.

Nevertheless, Dr. Bennett's figures suggest that the United Nations statisticians spoke more truly than they realized in mentioning the difficulty of computing reliable income figures for the underdeveloped countries. For these countries, the United Nations figures are possibly only one-third as large as they ought to be.

Despite the difficulties of making arithmetic computations, however, it would seem safe to say that half of mankind receives per capita incomes equal to less than 10 per cent of the American level.

A GEOGRAPHICAL COMPARISON

Table 7 presents the 70 countries in the United Nations tabulation, grouped by size of per capita income and by regions. It

* *Op. cit.*

TABLE 7. SEVENTY COUNTRIES CLASSIFIED BY SIZE
OF PER CAPITA INCOME IN 1949 AND BY REGION

Per Capita Income (U.S. dollars)	Europe	Asia	Latin America	Africa	Other Regions
Over $900					U.S. [a]
500–900	Switzerland Sweden United Kingdom Denmark Norway Belgium Luxembourg Netherlands				Canada New Zealand Australia
300–500	France Iceland Ireland Czechoslovakia Finland Germany Western Zone Soviet Union Poland	Israel	Argentina Uruguay Venezuela		
200–300	Hungary Portugal Italy Austria		Cuba	Union of South Africa	
100–200	Yugoslavia Greece	Turkey Lebanon Japan Syria	Chile Panama Colombia Costa Rica Mexico Brazil Peru	Southern Rhodesia Egypt	

[a] $1,458.

41

TABLE 7.   (*Cont.*)

Per Capita Income (*U.S. dollars*)	Europe	Asia	Latin America	Africa	Other Regions
$50–100		Iran Iraq Ceylon India Pakistan Afghanistan	El Salvador Nicaragua Paraguay Honduras Guatemala Dominican Republic Bolivia		

Under $50		Philippines
		Saudi
		  Arabia
		Yemen
		Burma
		Thailand
		Korea
		  (South)
		China
		Indonesia
			Ecuador
			Haiti
				Ethiopia
				Liberia	

Source: Statistical Office of the United Nations, *op. cit.*

shows that, next to the United States, the prosperous regions include three British Dominions and much of western Europe. No countries in Asia, Latin America, or Africa are in the "prosperous" group.

Upper-middle standards of living ($200 to $500 per capita) are enjoyed by 12 European countries, one Asiatic (a new nation, in Asia, many of whose inhabitants, however, came from Europe) four Latin-American countries, and one African—where much of the income is received by persons whose forebears came from Europe.

Below this level come the middle, lower-middle, and poor countries—including most of Latin America and Africa and virtually all of Asia.

THE POSITION OF THE WELL-TO-DO COUNTRIES

The well-to-do countries already have attained fairly good living standards and seem destined to enjoy further gains. Much of what has been said about the probable future progress of the United States applies to these countries also. It may be confidently forecast (if war does not interfere) that real incomes in most of western Europe, in Canada, New Zealand, and Australia will be greatly increased in future decades—perhaps doubled in the next half century.

THE SITUATION OF THE POOR COUNTRIES

The poverty of the nations other than those mentioned is due to the *supply* factor—low productive capacity—not to inadequate demand. Indeed, in some countries in recent years, China and Japan for example, there has been an excess of monetary purchasing power, with price inflation resulting. In most of the world the basic economic problem is *how productive capacity can increase*. Current output is low because the conditions of basic prosperity are unfavorable.

The first of these conditions, as noted in the preceding chapter, is the productive efficiency of the working population. The principal factors which affect the workers' productive efficiency were listed above as being these:

1. Education
2. Industriousness
3. Status of labor-management relations
4. Incentives
5. Restriction of output
6. Effective use of the work force
7. Sobriety
8. Honesty
9. Health

Of these conditions, the one that is clearly detrimental to the well-being of the underdeveloped countries is lack of education. The other factors are unfavorable in some places.

Table 8 shows the relationship between education and per capita incomes. The relationship, in general, is this: The higher the per capita income, the larger is the proportion of children in school.

TABLE 8. EDUCATION AND PER CAPITA INCOME
IN 70 COUNTRIES

COUNTRY	PER CAPITA INCOME 1949	PERCENTAGE OF CHILDREN 6–21 ENROLLED IN SCHOOLS AND COLLEGES
United States	$1,453	78.5
Canada	870	72.7
New Zealand	856	63.2
Switzerland	849	57.2
Sweden	780	36.1
Great Britain	773	64.6
Denmark	689	61.6
Australia	679	64.9
Norway	587	42.9
Belgium	582	60.3
Luxembourg	553	a
Netherlands	502	56.8
France	482	65.7
Iceland	476	a
Ireland	420	58.0
Israel	389	a
Czechoslovakia	371	53.0
Finland	348	44.2
Argentina	346	45.4
Uruguay	331	33.9
Venezuela	322	21.1
Germany	320 [b]	57.0

Note: See footnotes at end of table, p. 46.

TABLE 8. (Cont.)

Country	Per Capita Income 1949	Percentage of Children 6–21 Enrolled in Schools and Colleges
Soviet Union	308	66.5
Poland	300	52.1
Cuba	296	36.2
Hungary	269	32.6
South Africa	264	32.3
Portugal	250	25.5
Italy	235	43.5
Austria	216	a
Chile	188	41.0
Panama	183	31.6
Yugoslavia	146	33.8
Colombia	132	28.1
Greece	128	44.6
Costa Rica	125	33.3
Turkey	125	17.5
Lebanon	125	a
Mexico	121	31.2
Brazil	112	22.6
Southern Rhodesia	101	28.0
Egypt	100	21.1
Japan	100	52.2
Syria	100	26.2
Peru	100	21.3
El Salvador	92	16.2
Nicaragua	89	17.2
Iran	85	7.7
Iraq	85	9.6
Paraguay	84	39.7
Honduras	83	14.5
Guatemala	77	12.0
Dominican Republic	75	a

Note: See footnotes at end of table, p. 46.

TABLE 8.   (*Cont.*)

COUNTRY	PER CAPITA INCOME 1949	PERCENTAGE OF CHILDREN 6–21 ENROLLED IN SCHOOLS AND COLLEGES
Ceylon	67	*a*
India	57	12.0
Bolivia	55	14.0
Pakistan	51	*a*
Afghanistan	50	4.8
Philippines	44	33.6
Ecuador	40	29.5
Saudi Arabia	40	*a*
Yemen	40	*a*
Haiti	40	9.4
Ethiopia	38	*a*
Liberia	38	2.4
Burma	36	*a*
Thailand	36	28.1
Korea	35 *c*	18.1
China	27	11.4
Indonesia	25	*a*

a Figures not available. *b* Western Zone. *c* Southern.

SOURCES: Of the income figures: Statistical Office of the United Nations, *op. cit.* Of the enrollment figures: R. M. Hughes and W. H. Lancelot, *Education: America's Magic* (Ames, Iowa: Iowa State College Press, 1946), pp. 178–181. (The enrollment figures are for various years from 1931 to 1940, but most of them are for 1936–1938.)

The causal connection runs two ways: 1. The wealthier a people, the more education they can afford to give their children and 2. The more education the children get, the more productive and the wealthier they will be when they become income-earning adults.

The education figure for Soviet Russia seems to be unusually high. It may be an exaggeration, as are so many of the Soviet Government's statistics. If, however, the *quantitative* education figure is not inaccurate, the comparatively low-income figure testifies to the low *quality* of Russian education. In Russia, education is a propaganda instrument—a mixture of truths, half-truths, and untruths.

As a professional educator who has studied carefully the various elements bearing on economic well-being of nations, the author believes it advisable to call special attention to the importance of *good* education as a key contributor to economic progress.

Providing education, however, is a costly task. Before World War II, the United States was spending between $2.5 and $3 billion of public money a year on education. This figure represents public outlays and does not include tuition fees or the personal expenditures of the students, which are largely paid for by their families. In 1948–49, public expenditures on education amounted to $5.5 billion. This figure represents about $37 per capita of the total population.

The per capita incomes of the people of India and China are hardly adequate to feed and clothe them, to say nothing of providing a surplus for supporting more education while simultaneously releasing their children from productive work in the fields.

The inadequacy of free education in the poorer countries helps to explain also the absence of economic mobility and the widely prevalent state of poor health. Absence of or inadequate medical care and lack of or unsatisfactory public health programs conduce also to poor health and disease. Like education, however, adequate medical and health programs are costly.

NATURAL RESOURCES AND POPULATION

The second important factor in per capita productivity is the relationship between the quality and quantity of natural resources and the size of the population.

The population question may be stated as follows: A region may be either too sparsely populated for effective economic organization or so densely populated that the nation's economy is pressed far into the area of diminishing returns. It is doubtful that poverty of large countries is caused by sparsity of population. On the contrary, many areas of China and India are overpopulated. In these areas an increase in productivity is possible—by using better methods and more capital equipment and by raising better food products. If such improvements, however, were to be accompanied by disproportionate increases in the population, the potential gain in per capita production would not be completely attained. Indeed, if the population growth were swift enough, there would be no rise whatsoever in output per worker—the results of technological improvements would have been swallowed up by more mouths rather than yielding more per mouth. The population factor in many of the poorer nations, therefore, must be counted as very important in determining the standard of living.

BUSINESS MANAGEMENT

Skilled business managers are scarce in the poorer countries.* The opportunities for men to learn to be good business managers are almost nonexistent. The educational systems are inadequate; agricultural extension services (to aid farmers) are virtually nonexistent; there are relatively few business schools or businesses and industries in which men can learn management skills on the job.

One reason for the scarcity of competent business managers in many countries is a condition perhaps hard for Americans to comprehend—*the low social position of businessmen.* In most countries the top social position is accorded to the people who *do not have to work at all*—the nobility and the landed gentry. Next come the military and the priestly classes. Government officials, lawyers, and physicians usually enjoy high social status. Businessmen, by contrast, enjoy little or no social standing in

---

* This statement is not based on statistical evidence but rather on the writer's observations in 24 other countries.

most countries and may actually be looked down upon as scoundrels and knaves.

In most lands outside the United States, bright young men who take account of the social standing of the various occupations in deciding which one to enter tend to avoid business. This means that talent is repelled from business management.

Contrast this with the situation in the United States. Who are the nobility? They are the "steel kings," the "lumber barons," the "merchant princes," the "lords of finance," the "captains of industry." Bright young Americans are not deterred from going into business by social factors. On the contrary, business success is as good a path as any to social standing and public esteem. Moreover, American universities, laying aside the Old World attitude toward commerce and industry, have taken the eminently sensible step of making the study of business administration a division of higher education. These various factors help to explain why the United States has so many competent business managers and so many well-run, productive business enterprises.

CAPITAL GOODS

Perhaps the most easily seen and most clearly measurable factor that holds down per capita production in much of the world is inadequacy of capital goods. In the poor countries, farm equipment is primitive; factories are few; and power-driven machinery is scarce. Table 9 illustrates the relationship of these conditions.

The principal explanation of the world scarcity of capital is, paradoxically, the poverty of the people. The provision of capital requires saving and investment. Most of the peoples of the world have barely enough income to live and have no surplus available for saving. Incentives are not lacking—capital earns a high return because it is so scarce. Invention, research, and the development of capital equipment are scarce because of the lack of technical training and enterprise necessary to such achievement.

TABLE 9. POWER CONSUMPTION AND PER CAPITA INCOMES IN 54 COUNTRIES, 1949

COUNTRY	PER CAPITA POWER CONSUMPTION (*Coal equivalent, in pounds*)	PER CAPITA INCOME
United States	15,975	$1,453
Canada	13,840	870
United Kingdom	9,460	773
Norway	8,650	587
Belgium	7,590	582
Sweden	6,205	780
Australia	6,405	679
Iceland	6,580	476
Czechoslovakia	6,160	371
Germany (Western Zone)	5,325	320
New Zealand	5,195	856
France	4,885	482
Switzerland	4,160	849
Denmark	3,740	689
Poland	4,270	300
Netherlands	4,025	502
Union of South Africa	4,115	264
Austria	3,235	216
Finland	2,135	348
Ireland	2,110	420
Hungary	2,070	269
Israel	1,385	389
Argentina	1,560	346
Chile	1,740	188
Japan	1,670	100
Southern Rhodesia	1,410	101
Italy	1,275	235
Uruguay	1,300	331
Mexico	1,340	121
Cuba	1,055	296
Yugoslavia	790	146
Colombia	660	132

TABLE 9.   (*Cont.*)

COUNTRY	PER CAPITA POWER CONSUMPTION (*Coal equivalent, in pounds*)	PER CAPITA INCOME
Panama	680	183
Portugal	550	250
Turkey	595	125
Costa Rica	485	125
Greece	460	128
Brazil	440	112
Peru	460	100
Ecuador	330	40
Iraq	350	85
Guatemala	310	77
Honduras	330	83
Egypt	310	100
India	220	57
Ceylon	175	67
Bolivia	155	55
Nicaragua	155	89
El Salvador	130	92
Indonesia	90	25
Pakistan	90	51
Burma	45	36
Haiti	45	40
Thailand	20	36

SOURCES: Of the power figures: W. S. and E. S. Woytinsky, *World Population and Production* (New York: Twentieth Century Fund, 1953), p. 941. Of the income figures: Statistical Office of the United Nations, *op. cit.*

Providing capital equipment for a poor world requires immense resources. In the United States the capital investment per worker is at least $7,000. China's population figure suggests that there are some 200,000,000 Chinese workers. To provide them with capital equipment equal to only $1,000 per worker would require $200 billion. To provide them with $7,000 of capital per worker would take $1,400 billion, or $1.4 trillion!

ENTERPRISE

Enterprise seems to be at a low level in most of the poor lands. The spirit of enterprise depends greatly on subtle psychological factors associated with the customs and attitudes of peoples. In the poorer countries, custom, inertia, and tradition oppose the development of that "divine discontent" which is essential to progress. Since education encourages ambition and stimulates imagination, the inadequacy of education is an important explanation of lack of enterprise.

THE ROLE OF GOVERNMENTS

The governments of the poor countries do not contribute greatly to economic well-being. Some governments—national and local—are inefficient, corrupt, or both. In general, the genuinely democratic governments seem to do a better job economically than do either dictatorships or governments that are ostensibly but not really democratic. Perhaps this is because democratic governments adopt fewer unwise policies. Surely it is partly because genuinely democratic governments are oriented more toward the masses of the people, whereas other governments are likely to favor a handful of "upper class" people. The more genuinely democratic a government, the more it is likely to be concerned with the development of the entire human resources of a nation.

ANALYSIS BY GROUPS

Analysis of two groups of countries—the richest and the poorest—as presented in Table 7, page 41, reveals some differences that are interesting and that may also be significant.

Consider first the countries that (relatively at least) may be described as prosperous—the 12 having per capita incomes higher than $500. They share certain characteristics. All these countries are:

1. Either in western Europe, or their peoples are predominantly of western European descent
2. Countries in which the predominant religion is Christianity
3. Located in the Temperate Zone
4. Democratic countries

Consider on the other hand the poor countries—the 40 having per capita incomes lower than $200. Of these countries it may be said:

1. None is a western European country, and very few of their inhabitants are of western European descent.
2. Some are Christian countries, but in most of these nations the people predominantly belong to the other great religious faiths—Mohammedanism, Buddhism, Confucianism, Hinduism, and the other major groups.
3. Some are in the Temperate Zone; some are not.
4. Very few could be described as genuinely democratic countries.

FACTORS UNDERLYING THE CAUSES OF POVERTY

In this chapter we have noted the poverty of most of mankind and its proximate cause—low output per man-hour. Pushing the analysis farther, we have sought for the causes of this low output and have found them in shortages of trained workers, of capital goods, of skilful management, and of enterprise; in underdevelopment of natural resources; in some instances in overpopulation; and in ineffectiveness of governments.

Turning our attention to the causes behind these causes, we may ask, "Why do these conditions prevail?" Consideration of this question takes us into deep waters. We have to turn attention to the subtle and complex psychological and social factors that are called the *mores* of peoples—their basic customs, habits, ways of thinking, emotional attitudes, and behavioral patterns.

This job is the task of the psychologist, the sociologist, and other scientists. The economic analyst may venture only to suggest certain factors that may be worthy of consideration in explaining the causes behind the causes of the immense difference between the performance of the people of the United States and of other well-to-do nations on the one hand and that of people in the poor countries on the other.

1. *Hard work among the well-to-do.* Poor men in all parts of the world work hard. In many nations, however, the "upper classes" despise work and aim to do as little as possible. In the United States, however, even the rich men and the captains of industry work hard. It is the national custom. The result is that our top talents are not lost by loafing, but rather they are busy helping to enlarge national production.

2. *"Divine discontent."* This arresting phrase of Kingsley's helps to explain progress. In countries where the people are satisfied with things as they are or are so unimaginative that they do not realize that things could be better, there is little progress. In the United States, however, the philosophy "bigger and better" is sufficiently pronounced to have attracted the scorn of some observers—especially those who like to make fun of the United States. In fact, however, this spirit, which makes every American a potential inventor, improver, and innovator (and an actual one in many cases) is a key factor in explaining American progress. Americans have a restless urge to do things quicker, better, cheaper—often inventing machines to achieve these ends.

3. *Competitive spirit.* From the earliest years—the years that child psychologists say basically mold the adult—American children, in play and school, participate in activities that have a large element of competitive spirit. Many games, both of youngsters

and of adults, are entirely competitive—they offer competition for its own sake. Competition is a valuable spur to economic progress, and the vigor of the competitive spirit in the mores of the American people helps to explain that *urge to excel* which powers so many economic advances.

4. *Religion.* Christianity seems to be favorable to economic productivity.

5. *Climate.* A cool climate, rather than a hot or a cold one, seems to be a factor of some importance but not a vital one.

6. *Ethnic group.* The Western European peoples seem to have developed characteristics favorable to economic progress to a larger extent than have most other groups.

"INDUSTRIALIZATION" NOT THE WHOLE ANSWER

Generally speaking, the higher the standard of living of a country, the smaller is the proportion of its workers engaged in agriculture and the greater the proportion of its people occupied in manufacturing, trade, commerce, transport, and other non-agricultural pursuits. These facts seem to have led some persons to believe that the way for the poorer countries to raise their income levels is by industrialization.

The suggestion is sound, in part, but it is also misleading. It is misleading because the plan would not work for all of the poor countries simultaneously unless at the same time they also increased their agricultural output per farmer.

It is true that if *one* poor country (or even a few) were to follow this path, their endeavors could be successful, under certain conditions.* These conditions can be illustrated by thinking of

* There are two other exceptions to the proposition, both of them probably of minor significance. 1. If the industrialization takes the form of making, not automobiles and radio sets, but rather of producing appropriate agricultural tools, food output may be increased by diverting labor into such factories. 2. Food output will not be reduced if farmers can be employed in factories at times of the year when they would otherwise be doing little or nothing.

the typical poor country in which most of the workers are in agriculture. Suppose now that the country were to become industrialized, producing manufactured goods cheaply. If the country could export a sizable proportion of these goods in exchange for foodstuffs, it could have as much food as before and, in addition, more manufactured goods. But the newly imported foodstuffs would be coming from other lands whose peoples would have less to eat than before unless their agriculture had been improved simultaneously.

In short, if *all* the poor countries are to have *both more to eat and more of other goods also,* they cannot divert workers from farms to factories unless they increase the output per farm worker. An improvement in agricultural methods is an essential for the poor countries. If agriculture is improved in such countries, they can release productive resources to be used in producing manufactured goods.

The development of the United States illustrates this proposition. The productivity of American agriculture has increased rapidly—so rapidly indeed that the American farm problem is not the Malthusian one of pressure of the population on the food supply but rather one of pressure of the food supply on the population. This rise in agricultural productivity has permitted a steady rise of urbanization and industrialization, and also a larger food supply. Similarly, world prosperity will require industrialization, but industrialization will be impossible except as per capita agricultural output is raised. Then the entire world can have both more food and more manufactured goods.

AN OVER-ALL VIEW

In the poor countries the economic problem is not that of maintaining full employment; there never is much unemployment in such predominantly agricultural countries. The real economic problem in these countries is how to raise per capita output. Their peoples are poor because the average man produces so little. The solution to this problem lies along lines of improving techno-logical processes, of securing mechanical equipment, of educating the people, of securing efficient farm and industrial management, and of using effective production methods. These are the ways in which the peoples of the poor countries can advance to a higher standard of living, a goal which all men of good will must enthusiastically approve and be willing to assist.

The statement of this problem and the nature of its solution, however, should make it immediately clear that the economic problem in the high-standard countries is substantially different. In the United States the productive capacity is not low. In fact, output per man-hour is so extraordinarily high that the real problem is how to provide enough monetary demand to buy all the goods that all the workers can produce, thus keeping them all employed.

WHAT CAN THE UNITED STATES DO TO HELP?

The American people would like to help the peoples of the world achieve a decent standard of living. Naturally we do not wish to impoverish ourselves by such a program of assistance, nor, indeed, should we do so, for that would be a mistake from their point of view as well as from ours.

Consideration of the causes of low productivity makes it clear that economic salvation rests basically with the poorer countries themselves—they must raise their own per capita production. In other words, the rich countries cannot produce the goods which the poorer countries need; the most that the advanced countries can do is to help the others produce for themselves. Any program under which the United States or other nations plan to advance money or assistance of various kinds to other countries should be evaluated in the light of these basic facts.

A list of the factors which make for low per capita production must make it absolutely clear that there is unfortunately no magic formula or mysterious secret which can produce an overnight multiplication of production. Increases in capital equipment, in technological "know-how," in education, in skillful business management, and, in addition, the development of a progressive spirit are the work not of months or even years, but rather of decades.

To these developments, the United States and other countries can contribute much. We can lend money to buy capital equipment. (Indeed, that is much easier than teaching untrained, uneducated men to *use* the machines carefully and effectively.) We can send experts to teach technology, and we can train experts and teachers from these countries in our farms, factories, and schools. We can do these and other things—all directed at the basic objective of helping people to help themselves.

The foregoing suggestions deal with raising the per capita output of the poor nations. There is one other thing, and it is by far the most important thing which the United States can do to assist world prosperity—that is to maintain American prosperity at a high level. When the United States is prosperous, we offer a large and profitable market for the goods of many lands—the rubber of the East, coffee from Brazil, wool from Australia, burlap from India, sugar from Cuba, and furs, liquors, lumber, woodpulp, newsprint, and literally thousands of other items from all over the world.

When business is good in the United States, these commodities sell in large volume at profitable prices; they contribute substantially to the prosperity of the exporting countries.

When, however, a depression occurs in our country, the sales and the prices of these goods fall. These declines may be serious to the exporting countries. Indeed, sometimes the result is catastrophic. Monetary systems of those countries are upset, and often their governments fall. Economic unrest and political confusion follow. Radical agitation flourishes.

Clearly, then, one of the most important things that the United States can do for world prosperity and stability is to keep itself prosperous.

CAN THE UNITED STATES BE PROSPEROUS BY ITSELF?

As much as we would like to see the standard of living of the peoples of the world rise rapidly to the comfort level, it is clear that the process will require many years, perhaps decades. The fact that the economic fabric of the world is so closely interwoven may raise the question of whether or not the American people can achieve the ever-higher standard of living which is forecast in this book. Is our prosperity so closely tied to that of the rest of the world that we cannot go ahead faster than the other countries do?

Fortunately the answer to this question is perfectly clear—the United States can advance just as rapidly as our brains and energy permit; we shall not be held back in the least by less progressive countries. The people of the United States are, and for many decades have been, more prosperous than the people of other countries. Our prosperity rests basically on our high per capita production, which is something that poor India and poor China cannot take away from us, or even threaten. The average American farmer and industrial worker, with the aid of modern equipment, good organization, education, and effective methods, produce a large amount of food and goods. Moreover, these favorable factors are continually improving. There is a marked upward trend in per capita output. The trend will continue. Our children and our children's children will enjoy a much higher standard of living than we do, *no matter what happens to the standard of living of the poor countries.*

We hope that the poor countries will make rapid strides, and we should do everything reasonable to help them to advance; it is not true, however, that our own progress and level of well-being are tied to theirs. Our prosperity can advance as rapidly as we can make it do so.

SUMMARY

1. The income levels of the peoples of the various nations range from mere subsistence to comfort.

2. The level of income depends on the level of output.

3. The size of output depends on productivity, and this, in turn, is controlled by many different factors.

4. In the poor countries the controlling factors, in the aggregate, are unfavorable but in the rich ones, favorable.

5. We have examined the causes behind the causes and have considered ways of improving these conditions.

========= CHAPTER 5 =========

England—A Case Study

THE DEVALUATION OF THE ENGLISH POUND TO $2.80 IN SEPTEMBER, 1949 symbolized dramatically the difficulties of a great nation. An analysis of these British difficulties is of double interest to Americans—first because of our natural interest in this great and friendly nation and people, and secondly because of the significance that England's experience may have for us.

Before our discussion of Britain's problems, a word of caution is necessary. Currently it seems that many commentators have exaggerated notions of the plight of England and of the magnitude of her difficulties. From these observers one might gather the impression that the United Kingdom is going downhill economically, or even that she is virtually finished as an industrial power.

This concept of the situation, however, is inaccurate. Britain has progressed greatly in past decades and has been making good headway since World War II. In 1949, the United Nations figure for the per capita real income of Britons was about one half of that of Americans—$773 compared with $1,453. If this level seems low, let it be remembered that very few countries enjoyed a higher standard than did England. They were the United States, Canada, New Zealand, Switzerland, and Sweden. In short, among the countries of the world, Britain was one of the richest.

This showing is remarkable, considering the impact of World War II on British industry. Table 10 shows the unhappy effects of the war on England, as illustrated by the low figure for 1946, and the substantial recovery that was made in subsequent years.

TABLE 10.   INDUSTRIAL PRODUCTION IN THE UNITED
STATES AND THE UNITED KINGDOM,
SELECTED YEARS FROM 1937–1952

Year	United States	United Kingdom
1937	59	91
1938	46	86
1946	89	83
1947	97	89
1948	100	100
1949	93	106
1950	108	114
1951	115	117
1952	119	114

Sources: 1937–1948: United Nations, *Statistical Yearbook, 1952* (New York: United Nations, 1952), pp. 87, 97. 1949–1952: United Nations, *Monthly Bulletin of Statistics*, Feb. 1954, p. 24.

In an analysis of the English economy the question, therefore, is *not:* Why has England collapsed? The problem, rather, is: Why is her position not more satisfactory than it currently is?

This chapter is devoted to this simpler and happier question. The analysis starts with a short historical summary of modern England's development and then considers the factors that have retarded her progress in recent decades.

Consideration of these factors is significant for Americans. Our country is in many respects in a position similar to that of Britain's a century ago. We would do well, therefore, to study carefully the English experience and to consider whether any of the conditions that have hampered her rate of progress exist in our country, or might arise in the future. Britain represents a case study of a more mature economy, and analysis of her experience sheds light on the causes of economic progress.

THE GROWTH OF ENGLAND

The Industrial Revolution made England the world's first industrial nation and started her on the road to world dominance, a position that she held for a century. The amazing improvements in machinery and manufacturing methods that began in England in the eighteenth century enabled her to produce goods cheaply. Subsequent improvements in ocean transport made her goods available to the world. For many decades the world clamored for English goods; the world got them—carried in English ships, financed by English banks.

This industrial strength, her defeat of Napoleon, and her gift for colonial administration were some of the factors that brought Great Britain wealth, power, and empire.

Decades passed; the international system of selling raw materials to England and buying finished products from her appeared to be a part of the eternal order of things. Then, late in the nineteenth century, other nations started to industrialize rapidly, and some began to advance economically and technologically faster than England. Other countries introduced improvements in types of goods produced, in methods of manufacture, and in techniques of marketing. Germany, the United States, Japan, and other countries entered the export trade, wooing the markets of the world with new goods at low prices, with effective advertising and selling methods based on careful study of the wants of foreign buyers. These techniques have not in general been taken up by English manufacturers and exporters.

So strong, however, remained England's position that it was scarcely realized that important changes were occurring. Professor A. L. Bowley, the distinguished English economist and statistician, expressed what may have been a general English attitude at that time when he wrote these words in 1893:

Before we can admit that English foreign trade can be diminished, we must admit that foreign nations have sufficient capital and labor to spare (which in reality would take a generation or more to accumulate) to undertake our industries, that England can lose her compactness and her highly finished organization and multifarious division of labor, that English enterprise and courage is failing, that the energy, common sense and inherited skill of the English laborer is deserting him, that we have no resources but coal, can succeed in no manufacture but cotton, and shall lose command of the seas, and, more marvelous still, that some other nation will obtain and keep these advantages. The history of the nineteenth century teaches no such lesson.*

Despite this calm assurance it was no longer true that England had no rivals worth considering. Other countries were beginning to do their own manufacturing, and some were already exporting goods in competition with her. Other countries were being welded into strong nations—notably Germany, Italy, and Japan. Within the Empire, the dependencies were still loyal (as the events of two world wars were to show), but they were asking for more independence and self-government. In the distant west the United States was beginning to become more powerful. Indeed, Germany's ambitions and her naval building program unsettled the peace of Europe and were instrumental in leading to World War I.

After World War I, and despite the defeat of England's most aggressive rival, there was no reversion to the conditions of the nineteenth century. Germany turned out not to have been the villain of the piece after all, and England's dominance continued to decline. Britain's losses in World War II intensified her prob-

* Bowley, A. L., *England's Foreign Trade in the Nineteenth Century* (London: S. Sonnenschein & Co., 1893), p. 130.

lems, which were symbolized by the devaluation of the pound in 1949.

To summarize: the Industrial Revolution made England the world's first manufacturing nation, its greatest trader, and its pre-eminent financial power. Despite the "head start" and the overwhelming dominance, however, Britain did not maintain its lead. The historical sketch, above, sheds light on the ways in which Britain achieved its lead. We now turn attention to the conditions that have retarded her progress.

THE KEY FACTORS

1. Socialism. An explanation that has been heard frequently in the United States in recent years is that the socialistic policies of the Labor Government, after World War II, injured the English economy. Possibly they did. As shown in Table 10, industrial production in the United Kingdom rose 37 per cent from 1946 to 1950, as postwar recovery occurred. Perhaps the expansion would have been even greater if different policies had prevailed, but there is no denying the substantial progress in those years.

As a matter of fact, the socialization program probably is more a *result* of England's economic difficulties than a *cause*. The basic causes are older and deeper. Some of them started long before the Labor Party even existed. What, then, are these other factors?

2. Two wars. With the sole exception of Germany, the United Kingdom is the only country that fought the full duration of the two world wars. Her war losses were enormous. A large number of her finest sons lost their lives. Many of her ships were sunk. In World War II she sold billions of dollars' worth of foreign investments from which she formerly received income. Serious physical destruction of property was sustained from bombing. The adverse effect of these losses was immense.

3. Monetary policy after World War I. The first World War left Britain with a large national debt. For various reasons the

English government decided to re-establish the convertibility of the English pound at its prewar value of $4.86. This necessitated a deflationary monetary policy, which discouraged domestic economic activity and increased the burden of her domestic war debt. Decisions in the opposite direction would have been hard to take but might have been better for the nation.

4. *The loosening of the bonds of the British Empire.* First after World War I and again after World War II, the British dominions and colonies either acquired greater independence or separated completely from Britain. This process involved losses of employment and business to Britain.

5. *Taxation.* The combined taxes of national and local governments, after World War II, took about 40 per cent of the British national income. Taxation as heavy as this, together with the modest postwar level of incomes, was a deterrent to enterprise.

6. *The level of output per man-hour.* Most basic of all strands of explanation is the level of production per worker. As Colin Clark has shown,* output per man-hour has risen fairly steadily in Britain through the years. Figures on the real national product since World War II show that it is still rising. Nevertheless, British production per worker is lower than the American figure and is also lower than the level which would give the English people comfort instead of austerity.

The level of output per man-hour is a proximate explanation of the standard of living of a people. This basic factor, however, itself needs explanation; we shall go on to consider the circumstances that have kept it from being higher.

7. *Antiquated machinery and methods.* England once led the world in the use of new machinery and the development of new production methods. She does not today; nor has she for several decades. This situation antedated World War I by many years. English technological progress, fastest in the world a century and

* Colin Clark, *The Conditions of Economic Progress* (Second edition, London: Macmillan, 1951), p. 63.

a half ago, has been relatively slow (with a few brilliant excep-tions) for a long time. Today, her farms and factories have a great deal of old machinery and equipment which handicap her workers and her industries.

8. *Attitude of labor.* Organized labor has occasionally resisted the introduction of labor-saving machinery and has occasionally limited the amount of output which a union worker is allowed to produce in a day. However appealing such policies may seem at times, they hurt a nation's competitive position and retard the rise in her economic well-being.

9. *Restricted competition.* English law does not forbid the kind of industrial combinations that are prohibited in the United States by the Sherman Act and other antitrust laws. Many English industries are cartelized, with a stipulated division of markets and with pricing agreements. Some of these arrangements, indeed, have been backed by the English government. Agreements to restrain competition are very comfortable, but they remove the powerful competitive pressures—to make improvements in ma-chinery and methods, to cut costs and prices, and to improve products.

10. *Social stratification.* Politically a real democracy, socially England is a stratified society, although less so than in the past. A child has little opportunity to rise above his parents' class. This tradition is so well established that many "lower class" parents commonly take it for granted that their children will not try to move upward in the social and economic scale. The children of poor parents can get elementary and secondary schooling, but it is difficult for them to go to college. Higher education is mainly the privilege of the well-to-do. Before World War II, only 3.6 per cent of English young people were in college, compared with 14.6 per cent in the United States.

The result is that Britain does not utilize fully the talents of "lower class" children. A poor boy, for example, may have the ability to become a great engineer, contributing to his own and his country's well-being, but lack of educational opportunity causes him to spend his life as a common laborer instead.

11. Decline in the spirit of enterprise. In recent decades, English industry seems not to have had the vigorous progressive leadership that it had one hundred fifty years ago. Perhaps this condition resulted from an altogether natural complacency induced by Englishmen's knowledge of England's pre-eminent position in the worlds of politics, finance, industry, and trade during the nineteenth century. The mountain came to Manchester for so many decades that its continued coming possibly came to be taken for granted. Sir Josiah Stamp, able English industrialist and financier, said bluntly before the MacMillan Committee: "I do think that we have definitely fallen behind in the industrial efficiency race in quite a number of industries. We have had such a start in the Victorian era that we have been really resting on our laurels too much." *

12. The "country gentleman" ideal. In many respects the English country gentleman ideal represents a noble attitude. The gentleman does not take advantage of the weak nor behave in an ungentlemanly fashion in any other way. He serves his government—local and national—honorably and effectively. From an economic viewpoint, however, it is significant that he does not engage in active business. He lives by farming his estate and on such money as he is allowed to inherit. Thus the energies and abilities of these competent men are not devoted to economic progress. The ambition of many a vigorous English businessman is to retire to the country, hoping that his son, grandson, or great-grandson may become a country gentleman. This process drains talent away from industry, as men turn to rural pursuits instead of continuing to manage progressive business firms.

13. The social position of businessmen. Throughout history, with few exceptions, the social position of businessmen has been

---

* *Minutes of Evidence Taken Before the Committee on Finance and Industry* (London: His Majesty's Stationery Office, 1931), Vol. I, p. 265.

low. The historical pattern, as noted in the preceding chapter, has been that social prestige was possessed by four groups: the nobility, the landowners, the warriors, and the priestly class. Britain conforms in general to this pattern. A young man who seeks a career which will not impair his social standing will consider the armed services, the church, the civil service, medicine, university teaching, the law and "merchant banking"—which means investment banking, but *not commercial* banking. Entry into business, however, will imperil his social standing. If a young man of the upper class goes into business, he is likely to be described by the standard sentence, "Oh, yes, poor Smythe, he had to go into trade." So strong were class lines and the prejudice against "trade" that Sir Thomas Lipton, though a personal friend of Edward VII, was never completely accepted socially.

The lines are somewhat weaker today, but they are still strong and definite. The result is that talented and ambitious young men avoid business careers, thereby subtracting real ability from business leadership.

*14. Business education.** As a consequence of the low social prestige attached to commerce, England has been slow to recognize that conducting a business is or can be "an intelligent occupation." The young man proposing a business career is recommended to secure "a good general education" or, alternatively, to graduate as a chemist or engineer. Although there is a British Institute of Management, it receives only lukewarm support from businessmen. There is little interest or enthusiasm among the higher levels in business for the study of the art and science of management. Whereas in the United States in 1951 there were 380,000 students at the university level taking "business administration" as their major subject, the provision of educational facili-

* I am indebted for this point to the English management expert, Col. Lyndall F. Urwick, who kindly read this chapter and suggested improvements. I hasten to add that this grateful acknowledgment does not imply complete agreement on the part of Col. Urwick with everything in the chapter.

ties in Great Britain for those who wish to study in this field is almost negligible. The two senior universities of Oxford and Cambridge do not teach the subject at all. The young man of ability contemplating teaching the subject as a career must face the fact that there is no academic position of even minor distinction which is open to him.

15. *Tariff policies in other lands.* As industries have grown or struggled to grow in other countries, they naturally have sought the protection of tariffs. For many decades nations all over the world have gradually raised their tariff barriers in order to keep out imported goods. The result has been to impede the English export trade.

16. *Tradition.* The habit of thinking and behaving in a traditional manner may be either favorable or unfavorable to economic progress. If, for example, a nation's traditions favor enterprise, innovation, and improvement, the traditions encourage economic development. If, on the other hand, the tradition takes the form of an exaggerated respect for the traditional ways of doing things, and, a fortiori, if it involves an actual *resistance to change,* the tradition impedes improvement.

The English have many wonderful traditions. The following are some of them: courage, tenacity, decency, honesty, and respect for law. They are noble national traditions.

There also seems, however, to be a strong liking for habitual and long-established ways of carrying on business operations. The customary methods seem to acquire respected status; indeed, almost reverence. As one example, consider the method of keeping books. For decades, English business accounts were entered by hand, in pen and ink, by bookkeepers sitting on stools at high desks. Eventually, ingenious *machines* were contrived, in the United States and elsewhere, to do this work—faster, cheaper, and more accurately. Their use spread rapidly in America, slowly in England. The author's inquiries in English banks (where the keeping of accounts—as in all banks—is a large activity) suggested no reason other than a preference for the traditional way of keeping the books.

A SUMMARY VIEW

The foregoing strands of explanation are suggested as shedding light on the underlying causes of England's current difficulties and as offering answers to the question: Why is England's position not better than it currently is?

England is continuing to progress. What of the future? What England needs is not austerity—but productivity. Will it be achieved? Knowing the fundamentally strong qualities of the English people, one must have confidence in England's future. Englishmen may use the classic phrase, "England will muddle through," but it is dangerous to think in terms of that phrase. It was not by *muddling* that England became great, but by energetic, progressive, opportunistic activity; it is not by muddling that England can improve her position, but rather by a renewal of vigorous enterprise.

THE LESSONS OF BRITAIN'S EXPERIENCE

The United States today is in somewhat the same position that England was in a century ago. A century ago, so strong was Britain's economy that a forecast of the change in her position and her recent problems probably would not have been believed. Only sixty years ago, as competent an analyst as Bowley seemed to have no hint of the trends. Some of the factors operating in the changing English scene were subtle and slow in their effects. Long years elapsed during which adverse changes occurred; these passed unnoticed, it seems, until two crises broke the spell.

If it can happen in Britain, it can happen in the United States. It is appropriate, therefore, to ask whether any of the adverse factors which have developed in England exist or may arise in America.

The United States was injured very much less than Britain by the two world wars. Our war debt, relative to national income, is less. Taxation, which took 40 per cent of the English national income, took 25 per cent of the American national income in 1949. These relatively satisfactory domestic conditions could be altered, perhaps gravely, by another serious war.

Output per man-hour is high and rising in the United States. Technological progress in the development of new commodities and in production techniques is rapid. Enterprise is vigorous. If these vital factors in progress are threatened, the threat still lies in the future, not in the present.

There is relatively less social stratification in this country; educational opportunities for the children of poorer parents are better and are constantly being improved. Businessmen enjoy high social standing and prefer to be active rather than to retire and clip coupons. These factors are favorable; the important thing is to keep them so.

The problem of the "drift toward socialism" in the United States causes great concern among many persons and deserves careful watching. So far, however, the functioning of the private enterprise system has not been noticeably injured.

In short, it appears that none of the causes of the British difficulties are visible in the United States, *at least at present*. This is no guarantee, of course, that these conditions or other adverse circumstances may not appear in the future. We turn attention in the next chapter to an analysis of American productive capacity, to the factors that have made it large, and finally to those that will stimulate or retard its growth in the future.

SUMMARY

1. England became the first great industrial country and long led the world in economic strength. Later on, her pre-eminence

declined, although she continued to be a rich and progressive country.

2. Why has not Britain progressed even faster in recent decades? Sixteen different reasons have been offered.

3. Finally, it was suggested that what has happened in England could happen in the United States. Thus far, similar trends do not seem to have emerged. However, since many of England's trends have been subtle and hard to measure, the United States will do well to watch carefully for similar changes.

===== CHAPTER 6 =====

The Growth of Productive Capacity in the United States

PRODUCTIVE CAPACITY IN THE UNITED STATES HAS INCREASED greatly, at a fairly steady rate, throughout the nation's history. Output per man-hour, per worker, and per capita of the entire population has risen rapidly. Consequently, real per capita income has grown. Its current level is the highest in our history and in the world.

This progress *can* and *will* continue if the conditions of production become increasingly favorable. A few years ago, however, some persons were saying that ours had become a "mature economy." Apparently the term, so used, did not mean merely that the American economy was well developed, no longer primitive. It seems to have meant that the economy was capable of little or no further growth and was approaching a sort of economic senility. Doubtless, this view stemmed from the experience of the "Great Depression." The drop in economic activity—in national output and national income—was so great at that time that it could easily have been mistaken for a change in the long-time trend.

In fact, however, the slump did not indicate a drop in the supply factors and productive capacity. Output per man-hour rose throughout the depression. The decline was caused by inadequate demand. When demand became adequate in the 1940's, production and national income rose to new heights. By 1947 the national income (after adjustment for the inflationary changes) had risen to the level indicated by a projection of the pre-1929 trend.

This trend will continue if conditions are favorable. If all goes well, by the year 2000 the country's population will be about three hundred million, national income some $1,300 billion, and average family income about $11,000. These dollar amounts are in money having the same purchasing power as the 1954 dollar. What the figures mean is that the average real per capita income in the year 2000 will be about two and one half times as high as in 1950.

This increase will occur if nothing happens to prevent a continuing improvement in the supply factors described in Chapter 3 that determine productive capacity. What is the outlook for them in the decades ahead?

THE PRODUCTIVE EFFICIENCY OF THE WORKING POPULATION

1. *Education.* The "little red schoolhouse" is one of man's greatest economic inventions. It is, of course, much more than an *economic* force. It has been basic also to the development of the American political and social systems. So great indeed are the contributions of education to the American way of life and so invidious the connotations of the adjective "red" these days, that perhaps the symbolic term should be changed to the "little red-white-and-blue schoolhouse."

Education improves the quality of work, of management, of investment, and of enterprise. Until very recent years the trend of American expenditures on education represented a gradually increasing percentage of the national income. During the World War II inflationary rise of prices and incomes, however, educational expenditures did not keep pace. In the school year 1948–1949, total public outlays for education amounted to $5.5 billion, equal to 2.5 per cent of the national income. This amount was less than the annual expenditure on any one of the following commodity groups: cosmetics, tobacco, or liquor.

Before the war, educational outlays had risen to nearly 4 per cent of the national income. In order to accommodate the increased number of children, to build schoolhouses, to train and employ more teachers, and to pay better salaries to teachers, a very large increase in educational expenditures is imperative. This will require higher taxes. Such tax money, however, may properly be regarded as an investment in future national prosperity.

2. *Labor-management relations.* The United States has been going through a period of "growing pains" in the development of collective bargaining. Some of the newer unions have not yet acquired a sense of security. Many managements have not yet learned to deal skillfully with organized labor. Moreover, the period of rapid union growth has been an abnormal one—several years of depression and unemployment followed by a period of inflation and a very high rate of employment.

Progress has been made, however—much more than is commonly realized. Since strikes represent conflict and conflict is news, strikes get into the newspaper headlines. Contrariwise, negotiated settlements have no dramatic appeal. This emphasis on industrial disputes, however, is not truly representative of the total picture of labor-management relations.

There are more than 50,000 management-labor contracts in the United States. The average length of these contracts is about two years. Hence, about 500 contracts are renewed in the average week. In the average week there will also be some strikes. The strikes get the publicity. The successful efforts of thousands of labor and management representatives in reaching agreement on the terms of new contracts are not mentioned. These men are making collective bargaining work, and they deserve the nation's appreciation instead of having their efforts overlooked.

There is room, to be sure, for further improvement in labor-management relations. The success of labor and management in increasing output per man-hour and dividing the increased income equitably will be a decisive factor in determining American prosperity in the future.

If education is expanded, if labor-management relations are improved, and if the American people continue to be industrious, the efficiency of the working force will continue to rise.

NATURAL RESOURCES

The American people have been outstandingly enterprising in developing the nation's natural resources. Land has been prepared for cultivation and then used; minerals have been located and extracted; timber has been cut; water resources have been harnessed and used.

At the same time, however, many natural resources have been neglected and despoiled. Rich lands have been "mined," and soil erosion has occurred; mineral wealth has been wasted; timber has been slashed and the slashings have burned; streams have been polluted and silted. So great, indeed, has been the use and spoliation of our natural resources that voices have been raised in alarm, warning that our national prosperity is seriously endangered.

These pessimistic views, however, seem to be greatly exaggerated. A continuation of past thoughtless practices, to be sure, might eventually cause difficulties. Fortunately, the dangers have been recognized, and conservation programs have been started.

Careful study of the marvels of scientific discovery has convinced the present writer that new and better resources and materials will be developed before any major resource is exhausted.

BUSINESS MANAGEMENT

Business management utilizes such highly developed skills that in many fields business administration has attained a professional status in this country. Colleges of business administration and many business firms offer opportunities for training. Meeting places for experts in the various management functions—production, personnel, finance, accounting, marketing, and others—are offered by many professional associations. Similarly, there are groups organized by type of business—banking, manufacturing, farming, retailing, and a host of others. The services of county agricultural agents are of great value in improving farming and livestock raising. In addition, many periodicals are devoted to management functions and others to various types of businesses.

The net result of all these influences, when they are coupled with the energy and ability of business managers and with the comparative absence of social stratification, is a steadily rising number of men trained in management skills. If the trend continues, as seems probable, these conditions will be favorable to an enlargement of prosperity.

CAPITAL GOODS

An outstanding characteristic of the American economy has been the increase in capital equipment, especially power-driven machinery, on farms and in factories. Within seven years, 1946-52, American industry invested $140 billion in new durable equipment and a few tens of billions in new plants. A continuation of investment in new and better buildings, machinery, and equipment will increase the output per worker.

Investment of available funds depends on the adequacy of incentives. Capital funds come principally from retained business earnings, from the sale of stocks and bonds, from bank credit, and from insurance funds.

The incentive that causes people to invest money is the prospect of a satisfactory return. Taxation of the return may reduce the incentive. A large part of corporation earnings is subject to double taxation—once when the profits are earned, under the corporation income tax, and again as personal income when they are paid out as dividends. In 1954 a modest reduction in this double taxation was made by Congress.

How greatly do present tax rates deter investment? This is a disputed question, and the actual evidence (as distinguished from mere assertions) is scanty. In view of the immense volume of capital investment that has occurred in recent years, it is appropriate to wonder whether investment would have been much higher during this period even if taxes had been lower.

A reduction in taxes is desirable, however, since it would both make more money available for consumption or investment and increase the incentive to invest. Increases in either investment or consumption, or both, could be expected to result.

Knowledge was referred to earlier as one of a nation's most precious capital assets. Research is the major method by which new knowledge is discovered. Educational institutions, businesses, foundations, and governmental units are some of the chief organizations which support and carry on resarch. The total of funds currently being spent on research is many times greater than the outlays before World War II. A continuation of a large industrial research program will contribute to increased future prosperity.

Specific ways in which some of these factors affect output per man-hour are listed in a survey of 133 manufacturing companies made by the National Industrial Conference Board.* This survey asked for a report on 1949 output per man-hour compared with that of 1948 and asked further for explanations of changes. A very few concerns reported that output was lower, but the overwhelming majority reported increases. Among the reasons given for increases were these: better machinery, better engineering, better efforts by employees, better management efforts, and improved methods, planning, equipment, and tools.

ENTERPRISE AND THE GOVERNMENT

Enterprise—doing new things—has long, perhaps always, been an American characteristic. Vigorous enterprisers have played a key role in the economic development of the nation, and the continued growth of the American economy will depend on the vigor of private enterprise.

The American economy has been developed primarily by the people rather than by the government. Private initiative and individual responsibility expressed by and shouldered by pioneers, farmers, workers, investors, businessmen—many of them to be classed as enterprisers—built the nation.

Simultaneously there occurred, on the part of the federal, state, and local governments, an immense development of governmental policies and activities affecting business. The past great growth of regulation, various proposals for new controls, and the high level of taxation have caused many observers to believe that the continued expansion of the private enterprise system is threatened and that the result is likely to be a weakening of that system, followed by the establishment of a socialistic system.

If this proposition is true, it is a matter of grave concern. Public opinion polls have shown that the American people are

* National Industrial Conference Board, *The Conference Board Business Record*, May 1950, p. 191.

overwhelmingly in favor of the private enterprise system and equally opposed to collectivism.

What evidence is there that the private enterprise system is being weakened? The extraordinary vigor displayed by the American economy in recent years is surely not the behavior of an economic invalid. The record-breaking levels of employment, national income, investment, and business profits would seem to indicate that recently the private enterprise system has been functioning better than ever.

From this it would seem to follow that although some governmental policies are unwelcome and may be unwise, they are not *threatening* the private enterprise system—not yet, at least. But it does *not* follow that all current governmental policies are sound. A vigorous private enterprise system can survive despite a few poor policies, but unsound policies are injurious nonetheless.

HOW GOVERNMENT CAN CONTRIBUTE TO PROSPERITY

Government can contribute to prosperity by preventing uneconomic actions of individuals and by giving appropriate encouragement to useful private activities. This means, primarily, carrying on efficiently the basic functions of government—protection of persons and property against violence; enforcement of contracts; prevention of fraud; protection of the public safety, health, and morals; provision of adequate education; creation of a proper monetary system; and protection against foreign enemies.

The secondary economic activities of government need careful scrutiny. These include regulation, subsidies, welfare programs, and the actual ownership and operation of business enterprises. The first three cost money, which requires taxation. When the government is actually in business, it may be competing with private enterprise, and any serious prospect of further expansion of governmental business activities is naturally unsettling to private business interests.

The degree of wisdom guiding governmental policies will be important to the future of American prosperity. How good these policies will be depends on many circumstances, including public opinion, the operations of pressure groups, and how the balance swings between disinterested knowledge and selfishness or ignorance. A friendlier cooperation among great groups such as government, business, labor, and agriculture in formulating sound public policies would be a valuable contribution to national progress.

MAINTENANCE OF COMPETITION

A basic tenet of the private enterprise system is *vigorous free competition*. Competition, however, is something that many persons believe in abstractly, especially for other people; however, as far as they themselves are concerned, they would prefer to have less competition. This preference, in the absence of restraint, may lead to agreements that restrict competition. The existence and vigor of competition depend partly on public policy—as expressed in laws and interpreted in the courts—and partly on the attitudes of businessmen. Businesses can make an important contribution to economic progress by competing fairly and vigorously.

The role of the government is to prevent unfair competition and restraints of competition. This responsibility involves the difficult and controversial subject of antitrust policy. Court decisions in recent years have been reinterpreting the Sherman Act and other statutes. The result is that great uncertainty prevails with respect to what are and what are not lawful business opertions. An important contribution to economic progress on the part of government would be a comprehensive and lucid restatement of the antitrust law which would remove confusion and effectively maintain competition.

TOWARD LOWER TAXES

When George Washington became President of the United States, annual federal taxes amounted to about 4 million dollars. In 1949, they were about 10,000 times as large. The national income had grown also. Nevertheless, in George Washington's time, federal taxes were only about 1 per cent of the national income, whereas in 1949 they took about 18 per cent of the national income. Combined federal, state, and local taxes took about 25 per cent.

That is a discouragingly high percentage for peacetime. Of course, 1949 was not a year of real peace. Nearly half of the federal expenditures was devoted to the armed forces and foreign aid, the latter being motivated in part by the same disturbed international situation that motivated the former. The Hoover Report * suggested that perhaps two or three billion dollars could be saved by more efficient organization and operation of the federal government. Further substantial reductions in federal expenditures would have to impinge on the military program, foreign aid, services to veterans, and/or agricultural subsidies.

Principally because of the Korea-stimulated armament program, federal budget expenditures rose to $66 billion in fiscal 1952 and to $75 billion in fiscal 1953. Federal budget tax revenue rose from $62 billion in fiscal 1952 to $65 billion in 1953.

The magnitude of this program led some to fear that we might be weakening our economy, or "bleeding the nation white," as the phrase went. Such an outcome would be welcome to the men in the Kremlin. In fact, however, these dismal results did not occur; they are not going to occur, nor will anything even resembling such sorrying conditions happen. In fiscal year 1953, American production reached a new high point. The heavy arms program may last a long time. If so, the high taxes will be un-

* *Fortune*, December 1949, p. 95.

fortunate, inconvenient, and a burden; however, they not only will not ruin the nation, but the nation will get stronger every year.

PRODUCTIVE CAPACITY AND CYCLICAL PROSPERITY

In this chapter has been presented an analysis of the conditions that will control the future productive capacity of the United States, together with suggestions for keeping these conditions favorable. If these factors are favorable, will the increase in productive capacity ensure that the United States will enjoy cyclical prosperity and freedom from future depressions? The answer must be in the negative. The improvements that raise productive capacity do not solve the business cycle problem—which is a matter of *demand*, rather than *supply*. These improvements increase supply, but they do not necessarily increase or stabilize demand. This country continued to experience an increase in productive capacity in the 1930's, and yet the Great Depression occurred, and actual production declined. Cyclical prosperity is a separate problem; indeed, it is likely that *the greater our productive capacity becomes, the greater becomes the difficulty of maintaining cyclical prosperity.*

The next part of this book deals with the problem of cyclical prosperity and expansion in the United States. The analysis has been restricted to the United States. This has been done, not because the problem is unimportant in other countries, but rather for the reasons following:

1. It is likely that a solution that is satisfactory for the United States would be of considerable value to other nations.

2. The United States is such a big factor in world economic affairs that American stability would contribute powerfully to world stability.

SUMMARY

1. The American people in past decades have experienced rising real incomes. This gain was made possible by the fact that national productivity grew faster than the population. This happened because the factors that control output per man-hour became increasingly favorable.

2. If these factors continue to be favorable, national productivity will he quintupled in the second half of the twentieth century, and population will double, thereby permitting living standards to rise to two and a half times their 1950 levels.

3. This increase in productivity, however, will create a problem —that of providing enough purchasing power to buy the rapidly increasing output of America's production machine.

4. If the purchasing power grows too rapidly or too slowly, the nation will experience inflation or deflation—the up's and down's of the business cycle. We now turn attention, therefore, to the business cycle and to the monetary factors that accompany it.

CHAPTER 7

Prosperity and Depression: Factual

THE MAINTENANCE OF AMERICAN PROSPERITY IS NATURALLY A matter of prime importance to the American people. But it is more than that. It is a matter of substantial concern to the world. This is because of the large role which the United States has come to play in world affairs, both in peacetime trade and in international affairs.

This role is the more important because of the world conflict between communism and the private enterprise system. This struggle for the possession of the minds of men bids fair to continue for a long time, and its ultimate outcome will depend to a considerable extent on the comparative success of the two systems in providing rising, stable standards of living.

If our country is able to stabilize its prosperity, American business stability will help greatly in maintaining cyclical prosperity throughout much of the world. Contrariwise, if the United States were to experience a great depression, many other countries of the world would be affected adversely. When the United States experiences a depression, the number and size of the export markets of many countries are reduced. The prices and sales of their export commodities decline as the American demand for imported goods drops off. Brazil is hurt because of the declining market for coffee; Cuba, because the price of sugar goes down; Britain, because sales of tweeds and cutlery decline; and so on through all the countries of the world whose people sell Americans any products whatsoever. American exports of capital are also reduced, with adverse effects on other nations.

Our country is in a position to do much to help the less advanced nations of the world to increase their productivity and thereby improve the standards of living of their peoples. This country has both knowledge and material resources on which to draw for the kind of assistance that will enable the peoples of the world to help themselves toward better living.

The maintenance of cyclical prosperity in the United States, then, will contribute to world prosperity in three ways:

1. It will aid cyclical stability in other lands.
2. It will provide the means that will enable us to assist other peoples in their economic development.
3. It will prevent political instability by demonstrating the effectiveness of the private enterprise system.

The maintenance of full employment and high production in the United States, therefore, is not a matter which is of interest to our own people alone. On the contrary, it is a matter of great importance to the world.

Before proceeding to a discussion of ways by which to achieve this goal, however, let us first discuss the factual background of business fluctuations and their nature and causes, in this and the next chapter.

EXPERIENCE TO 1929

Until the year 1929 the American economic system worked quite well. The historical record is one of dynamic growth and development. Indeed, the growth of our country was something to cause statistical wonder and legitimate national pride. In the year 1800 we were a small nation with a population of some 5,300,000 people concentrated almost entirely on the Atlantic seaboard. The total combined wealth of the American people at that time probably was about $600 million; their total combined income was probably no larger than this amount, and it may have been considerably smaller.

One hundred twenty-nine years later, in 1929, the population of the country had risen to 121,800,000 (estimated). The total wealth of our people, including both personal goods and the properties of public agencies and corporations, had grown to considerably more than $400 billion, while the combined income of all people in the United States was more than $87 billion.

In this 129-year period, to be sure, business conditions had their ups and downs. In earlier years, slumps were often called "hard times." In the latter part of the period, the term "business cycles" came to be applied to these fluctuations in general business conditions. The country's economic history records many depressions. Some were rather short, as in 1907–1909, and 1920–21. Some were long, as in the 1820's, the 1840's, the 1870's, and the 1890's.

THE GREAT DEPRESSION

Even the longest of the pre-1929 slumps, however, was mild and short compared with the depression beginning in that year. The 20-year period from 1929 to 1949 witnessed an enormous fluctuation in business activity. Table 11 shows the swings in the key business indicators during this period. The first years of the period witnessed the worst decline in our history and the last years, the greatest upswing.

Until 1929, we Americans, on the whole, were buoyant and optimistic about the future. What is more, our feeling had a good, sound basis. It was based on a long history of phenomenal eco-

TABLE 11. KEY FACTORS IN THE GREAT BUSINESS CYCLE, 1929–1948

Year	Amount of Money	N.Y. Times Index of Business Activity	Index of Wholesale Prices	National Income	Employment	Unemployment
	(Billions)	(1926 = 100)		(Billions)	(Thousands)	(Thousands)
1929	$ 55.8	110.2	95.3	$ 87.4	47,630	1,550
1930	55.2	97.1	86.4	75.0	45,480	4,340
1931	53.7	84.6	73.0	58.9	42,400	8,020
1932	45.7	72.1	64.8	41.7	38,940	12,060
1933	42.0	79.0	65.9	39.6	38,760	12,830
1934	49.0	82.9	74.9	48.6	40,890	11,340
1935	53.1	87.2	80.0	56.8	42,260	10,610
1936	58.7	99.0	80.8	64.7	44,410	9,030
1937	61.5	103.1	86.3	73.6	46,300	7,700
1938	60.0	88.5	78.6	67.4	44,220	10,390
1939	65.4	99.6	77.1	72.5	45,750	9,480
1940	70.7	108.2	78.6	81.3	47,520	8,120
1941	79.4	127.3	87.3	103.8	50,350	5,560
1942	86.1	133.1	98.8	137.1	53,750	2,660
1943	114.8	139.7	103.1	169.7	54,470	1,070
1944	141.6	145.3	104.0	183.8	53,960	670
1945	168.0	134.6	105.8	182.7	52,820	1,040
1946	176.2	130.5	121.1	180.3	55,250	2,270
1947	169.2	145.6	152.1	198.7	58,027	2,142
1948	172.9	149.2	165.1	223.5	59,378	2,064

Sources: For amount of money, wholesale prices, and national income, see Table 15, footnotes 4, 5 and 7, p. 133. N. Y. Times Index calculated from data sheets supplied by *The New York Times*. Employment and unemployment, *Statistical Abstract of the United States* (Washington: U.S. Government Printing Office, 1950), p. 175.

nomic progress that had brought to the average American the highest standard of living in the world—and at a rate of increase so rapid that a man could see it happening to him in his own lifetime. No wonder that Americans believed theirs to be the land of opportunity! The captain of finance who said, "Don't sell America short!" was not unique in his confidence; he merely expressed in stock market language a view probably shared by ninety-nine out of every hundred of his countrymen.

After 1929, however, our confidence and bold optimism were seriously diminished. The process of psychological collapse did not take place rapidly, however. On the contrary, it was slow. In 1930, many persons believed that the "recession" would be brief and unimportant. By 1931, however, the situation was serious, and by the end of the next year it was desperate. By the winter of 1932–33 there were fourteen million unemployed. Those who were employed worked short hours at reduced wages. The national income had dropped to $39.6 billion—less than half what it had been in 1929. The country may have been close to a social upheaval. Apparently the 1932 election provided an outlet for the public discontent, which was vented on the party then in power.

Then, in 1933, mounting desperation was checked as conditions began to improve. But, when the country went into another tail spin in 1937, before full recovery had been achieved (there were still eight million unemployed), the Great Depression was breaking its own record of length and severity. Different experts offered different explanations—some talked about national economic maturity, others about unsound governmental policies or economic inflexibility. Most men, however, probably were merely confused and wondered what was going to happen in the future.

THE EFFECTS OF THE WAR

In 1939, a series of vital and dramatic events began. War started in Europe in September. In the following year the American Defense Program was initiated. In the next year, on December 7, came the Japanese attack on Pearl Harbor and the entry of the United States into the war. Prior to December 7, 1941, defense spending (foreign and domestic) had already stimulated business activity noticeably. After Pearl Harbor, however, expenditures increased enormously, and the country's farms and factories gradually went into high gear. Despite the withdrawal, first of hundreds of thousands and then millions of the most physically fit men from production as they entered the armed forces, the great American economic machine moved up to higher and higher speeds. Month after month production records were broken, until by 1943 total industrial production was twice as great as in 1939.

There were plenty of jobs. Employment went up; unemployment went down. By 1943 there were only about one million unemployed, a number probably smaller than the normal minimum in a dynamic country. Production shot up—profits increased—incomes soared. The total national income, which had been $72.5 billion in 1939, rose rapidly and stood at $169.7 billion by 1943. Even after paying the higher war taxes and despite rationing, the American people were enjoying real prosperity for the first time in many years.

This war-boom prosperity did not, however, dispel the pessimism of the thirties. The pre-1929 confident optimism was not restored. People understood that the enormous war expenditures were producing a peculiar prosperity, but many doubted that prosperity would continue when the war expenditures ceased. Indeed, the prospective cessation of war expenditures became a grave cause for worry. Doubt, uncertainty, and even gloom about the future continued at about the same level as had been generated by the "Dismal Thirties." Indeed, these developments caused new confusion—people were puzzled by the fact that in wartime the nation was able to achieve a far higher level of prosperity than in peacetime.

As the war neared its close and the successful progress of our armed forces made it clear that victory was to be ours, both the man in the street and the experts began to worry about what would happen to the American business and industrial scene after the end of the war. The main facts were clear to everyone— on the one hand, the government was annually spending tens of billions of dollars buying the output of farms and factories. Most of this buying naturally would cease at the end of the war. On the other hand, there were some 12 million men and women in the armed forces, and most of these would be released and presumably would be seeking jobs.

These two factors—prospective reduction of government spending and demobilization of military personnel—caused many persons to believe that the period immediately after the end of the war would be one of widespread unemployment and low economic production. Estimates of the probable number of persons who would be unemployed a year after V-J Day varied widely. The lowest estimate was 8 million, and the predictions ran from that figure up to twice that number or more.

THE TRANSITION PERIOD

In actuality, these pessimistic forecasts turned out to be completely wrong. The transition period progressed very much better than anticipated. The number of unemployed, which had dropped below 1,000,000 during the war, rose only to 2,700,000 by March, 1946 and then started to decline.

Many factors accounted for the surprising situation in which unemployment, instead of rising to 8, 12, or 16 million during the transition period, went up to only 2.7 million. The principal factor was the immense postwar demand for goods. This demand was created by two factors—first, an actual physical shortage of goods which derived partly from the low production of the '30's and partly from the low production of civilian durable goods during the war. The second factor was that Americans, both individuals and corporations, had accumulated during the war an unprecedented quantity of liquid purchasing power. Wholly apart from war bonds and other liquid assets, the total amount of money in the country (currency plus bank deposits) had risen from $70.7 billion in June, 1940 to $168.0 billion in June, 1945.

This purchasing power—in the form of an immense demand for goods—was loosed upon the markets immediately after V-J Day, with the result that since businesses of all kinds were then able to sell more goods than they could possibly produce, they put out "Help Wanted" signs, hired demobilized veterans almost as rapidly as they left the services, and after a short delay began to produce civilian goods at a record rate.

The industrial production index declined sharply from its wartime high for a brief period—while factories were being converted from military production to peacetime goods, but even so, the temporary postwar low of the Federal Reserve index of industrial production—148 in February, 1946—was 38 points higher than the average figure for the peak year of 1929. By the following February (1947) the index was up to 185 and still rising. Touching 194 in October, it then leveled off.

In short, the transition period following V-J Day turned out—unexpectedly—to be a period of low unemployment, high production, and great prosperity. The total national income in 1946 was $180.3 billion, and in 1947, $198.7 billion. In the summers of 1947 and 1948 more than 60 million Americans were employed, not counting those in the armed forces—an all-time high.

POSTWAR INFLATION AND PROSPERITY

The enormous postwar demand for goods brought about not only full employment and high production, but also price inflation. During the war, price increases had been restrained by rationing and price control. Relaxation of these controls permitted the "repressed inflation" to explode into an actual, substantial rise in prices. The wholesale price index,* which had stood at 78.6 in 1940, rose to 169.8 in August, 1948, and then started to decline.

Employment and business activity also attained all-time highs. Employment averaged 47,520,000 in 1940; in 1948 it averaged 59,378,000. The New York Times business index, which stood at 108.2 in 1940, averaged 149.2 in 1948. The national income in 1940 was $81.3 billion—in 1948, $223.5 billion. Even after taking out the influence of price increases in these years, the growth in the real national income was more than 50 per cent.

A business recession beginning in the latter part of 1948 continued for about a year. Wholesale prices dropped 10 per cent, employment about 2 per cent, and industrial production 15 per cent. Unemployment rose rapidly, from 1,642,000 in October, 1948 to 3,576,000 a year later.

The business decline did not last very long, however, nor was it severe. By the end of 1949 the business indicators had stopped declining and had turned upward.

This business recession was not unexpected. On the contrary, it had been widely expected and talked about for some time. When it came, it was referred to as "the best advertised recession in history." Perhaps the really surprising thing about the 1949 dip was that it was so small. It would not have been amazing if people had reasoned thus: "Here is the decline that we have been expecting; now we must retrench." If, then suiting the action to the word, they had decreased their spending, the slump might have become serious. Actually, the only area in which there was a substantial drop in expenditures was that of business inventories of goods. Indeed, the drop in the value of the gross national product was almost entirely caused by a change from inventory accumulation to inventory reduction.

* 1926 equals 100.

SUMMARY

1. The economic history of the United States from 1800 to 1950 showed enormous growth, interrupted only by occasional slumps. Until 1929 depressions had occurred fairly frequently, but compared with the one that started in that year, the earlier slumps were mild.

2. The 1929–1933 decline was so great, and the period of depression for another eight years was so deep and so long that it looked to some persons as though the long-time growth trend of the United States had ended. This view was wrong. The nation's productive capacity had not stopped growing. Inadequacy of demand held actual production far below capacity output for long years.

3. The Great Depression was finally ended by the coming of war. How long would the depression have lasted if the war had not occurred? The evidence suggests that it would have continued for a long time. The needs of war finance forced high levels of government spending and monetary expansion. It is doubtful that any such program would have been possible in peacetime.

4. The lessons of the war's financial and economic experience will be discussed later, in conjunction with the analysis of the fiscal-monetary system, described in Chapter 13.

CHAPTER 8

Prosperity and Depression: Analytical

PLANNING A PROGRAM FOR PREVENTING DEPRESSIONS AND FOR stabilizing employment and production at a high and rising level necessitates giving attention to the nature and causes of changes in business activity. Having the causes in mind, we may then consider whether any of these forces can be reduced or eliminated. Some of the contributing conditions, as we shall see, can be mitigated. Others, however, could not be eliminated without injuring our economic system.

Fortunately, reliance does not need to be placed exclusively on eliminating the causes. It is also possible to use *counteracting* mechanisms designed to neutralize the influence of unstabilizing factors. Before proceeding, however, to a discussion of such mechanisms, let us examine the various circumstances that help to explain business cycles.

THE USE OF MONEY

A true business cycle can occur only in a complex economy, and a complex economy cannot exist without the use of money as a medium of exchange. The term, "a complex economy," refers to an economic system characterized by a high degree of specialization and division of labor. In such a system very few persons consume the goods that they themselves produce. The predominant pattern is one of labor working in specialized production, receiving money incomes, and spending the money for the products of other persons' work. In other words, almost all goods are *exchanged* after being produced and are then consumed.

These interrelated processes of highly specialized production and exchange of goods necessitate the use of a medium of exchange. In a simple society, of course, it is possible for a limited amount of specialization, accompanied by exchange of goods by *barter* to exist. Barter, however, is so limited in its possible use that the amount of specialization in a barter society is correspondingly limited. A modern industrial society would be quite impossible without the use of money.

In a primitive barter economy a true business cycle would not occur. It is true that such an economy might have good crop years and poor ones. Favorable periods might alternate with times of drought and famine. But the paradoxical feature of an industrial depression—involuntary unemployment of men and resources—would never be seen.

The use of money sets the stage for the appearance of business cycles. It would be conceivable, therefore, to eliminate business cycles by ceasing to use money. That move, however, would mean reverting to a primitive barter economy and a low standard of living. The cure would be worse than the disease. A better solution would be to strive for arrangements that would retain the advantages of the use of money while checking the fluctuations which its use permits.

FLUCTUATIONS IN EFFECTIVE DEMAND

In a country that uses money, production and employment depend on monetary demand, that is, on the willingness and ability of people to spend money. Individual businesses, as well as the total of business activity, rise or fall with the volume of spending. The three great streams of spending are payments for: 1. consumer goods, 2. capital goods, and 3. government purchases of goods and services. The manner in which these spending streams fluctuate is shown in Table 12.

TABLE 12.   GROSS NATIONAL PRODUCT
OR EXPENDITURE
(In Billions of Dollars)

	1929	1933	1948
Personal consumption expenditures	$ 78.8	$46.3	$178.8
Durable goods	9.4	3.5	23.5
Nondurable goods	37.7	22.3	102.2
Services	31.7	20.6	53.1
Gross private domestic investment	15.8	1.3	45.0
New construction	7.8	1.1	17.9
Producers' durable equipment	6.4	1.8	20.7
Change in business inventories	1.6	−1.6	6.5
Net foreign investment	0.8	0.2	1.9
Government purchases of goods			
and services	8.5	8.0	36.7
Federal	1.3	2.0	20.9
State and local	7.2	5.9	15.8
TOTAL	$103.8	$55.8	$262.4

SOURCE: *Federal Reserve Bulletin*, June 1950, p. 734.

Note: A large proportion of Federal Government outlays (for example, Social Security payments) does not represent direct purchases of goods and services but is classified as "transfer payments." These payments are income to the recipients—to be spent, saved, or invested by them.

These figures illustrate two key conditions which contribute to cyclical fluctuations:

1. The people (including individuals and corporations) are free to spend their money as they wish; they may spend more or less, as they see fit.

2. Not only are they free to alter their rate of spending, but in fact they do so, spending more at some times and less at others.

The first of these two conditions is an integral part of a free economy, a free country, and a free people. It is unthinkable, therefore, that any attempt to stabilize business should proceed along the lines of abridging the right of people to spend their money or not to spend it.

But within the exercise of that right, it is entirely proper to try to discover ways of stabilizing the *desire* to spend. Attention will be given to this problem presently. Before doing so, however, it will be useful to examine the conditions that lead to large fluctuations in spending.

INSTABILITY OF SPENDING

Fluctuations in business and employment are associated with fluctuations in effective demand. A slump occurs when spending —on consumer goods or capital goods—is reduced. What are the circumstances that cause fluctuations in spending?

With regard to *consumer goods*, the higher the real incomes of a people, the greater is the potential variability of expenditure. Poor people, living a hand-to-mouth existence, must spend their money as fast as it is received in order to buy the bare necessities of life. Such people have no choice as to whether or not to cut down expenditure; their expenses always equal or exceed their incomes. Rich people, however, have several ways of reducing their expenditures.

1. They may reduce the amounts they spend on comforts or luxuries—fancy food, clothing, clubs, travel, automobiles, jewelry, radios, furniture, and amusements.

2. They may spend less on necessary items and live by depleting their existing stocks. This can occur only to a small extent with respect to stocks of foodstuffs and the like. It can occur to a

larger extent if it takes the form of not buying clothing but wearing garments, shoes, and other things on hand to a greater or lesser degree of shabbiness; of not buying a new house or replacing the family automobile as soon as usual; and in general, of postponing expenditures on durable consumer goods.

3. If their prosperity has taken the form of considerable leisure time, they may cut their spending, without reducing their standard of living, by working in their (otherwise) leisure to produce for themselves things that they had been paying others to produce. Housewives may do the family washing instead of sending it to the laundry, make clothes for the family, bake bread and pastry, can fruits and vegetables, do their own domestic work, and so on. Men may tend vegetable gardens, do repair work around the house, or wash their own cars.

With regard to *capital goods*, the rule is that the more capital goods a nation has, the greater is the potential variability of spending. Businesses may reduce capital outlays in various ways:

1. They may permit their stocks of raw materials, supplies, and finished goods to decline—a reduction of inventories.

2. They may allow their fixed capital equipment to become depleted by failing to replace worn-out equipment, by not repairing equipment and plant—in short, by permitting physical depreciation or depletion, or both, while possibly accumulating funds against them.

The business cycle occurs principally in highly developed countries, although serious repercussions may be felt in less developed countries which export goods to the former. The richer a country is and the more capital goods it uses to aid its production, the bigger can be the general business fluctuations expected.

One way of reducing the swings of the business cycle, therefore, is to reduce our total of capital equipment and our standard of living. This solution, however, would be a sorry one. A better solution would be to stabilize capital expenditures at a high level.

In looking for ways of stabilizing consumer expenditures and capital outlays, it is useful to inquire *why* spending fluctuates so greatly.

CAUSES OF CHANGES IN SPENDING

Changes in *consumer* spending usually are caused by variations in the income of consumers. When employment and earnings rise, purchases of consumer goods increase, and vice versa. An upswing or downswing of business, therefore, is not ordinarily started by a spontaneous consumers' buying strike or by a consumers' buying spree, although such changes do occur occasionally.

Changes in *business* spending, however, seem to occur spontaneously. Businessmen are continually deciding whether or not to build new plants, buy new machinery, or expand or contract their inventories. In making these decisions, they weigh the outlook for sales volume, prices, taxes, profits, and other factors. If the business outlook seems bright, they go ahead. If, however, they are seriously concerned about future business conditions, they reduce their outlays. Changes in the state of business confidence translate themselves into changes in business spending and investment. For example, in 1948 business inventories were increased by $6.5 billion. The *annual rate* of increase in the fourth quarter was $9.0 billion. Then, businessmen appeared to become cautious. Inventory accumulation slowed down and was replaced by inventory depletion. In the third quarter of 1949, business inventories were *reduced* at at annual rate of $2.4 billion. Thus, in nine months, this part of effective demand declined by $11.4 billion (annual rate).

Another condition that makes for fluctuation in business spending is the irregularity with which major investment opportunities make their appearance. In a progressive, expanding economy there appear from time to time new business and investment opportunities, as new areas are developed, new commodities invented, or new methods of producing old commodities perfected. Outstanding examples of such opportunities in American history include the development of the great national railway network, the expansion of the electrical industry, the growth of the automobile and aircraft industries, and—more recently—the development of radio and television. Such innovations produce large openings for profitable investment.

The appearance of these new things for which to spend money, however, does not go on at a regular rate, nor does the disappearance of older products and industries. These phenomena may be visualized by imagining the factors contributing to the *rise* of some industry to be *white* beads on a string, the beads being proportioned to the size of the opportunity, while other circumstances contributing to the *decline* of specific industries are thought of as *black* beads strung on the same string. Then let us suppose that these beads, representing economic increases and decreases, are strung on a long string, representing the history of the United States. We would find that the beads would not be spaced at regular intervals, and we would see that the white ones and the black ones did not occur chronologically in such fashion as to offset one another precisely. We would note the phenomenon of "bunching." At times, a number of white beads (including some big ones) would be bunched together, accompanied by relatively few black beads. At other times, several big black beads would be bunched together with very few white beads scattered among them. When the white beads are bunched together, a net stimulus to business expansion occurs, but when the black beads are bunched together, business is likely to be depressed because of the simultaneous and unconnected appearance of adverse factors in several businesses at once. There is, of course, no way of preventing this irregularity. Such irregularity of appearance, both of favorable and unfavorable factors, is simply a part of the pattern of a free enterprise society.

SPENDING, SAVING, AND INVESTING

The principal way in which the use of money encourages business fluctuations is by making it possible for an individual to *save* without *investing*. He can do so simply by not spending all of his income, thereby accumulating cash—usually in the form of a bank deposit.

Not everyone, of course, wants to save; those who do may not want to save all the time. Some persons desire to *dis-save* (spend *more* than their incomes) or are forced to do so by circumstances. But on the whole, there is more saving than dis-saving. Moreover, this desire to save is fairly steady.

Cyclical instability has one of its principal causes in a dilemma involving two elements: 1. The comparative steadiness of the desire to save and 2. The unsteady willingness on the part of would-be savers to *invest* their savings, plus the unsteady willingness of other persons, e.g., corporation managers, to invest the capital funds which they control, raise, or borrow.

The people of the United States secure employment by employing one another. They employ one another as a result of spending money for goods and services. Individuals buy consumer goods—food, clothing, automobiles, etc. Businesses buy raw materials and equipment, build buildings, and hire laborers. The people as a whole, however, including the corporations, are also disposed to save, that is, not to spend the whole of their current incomes. How then, if the people wish to consume less than their current incomes, can they earn incomes in excess of what they pay others for current production? In somewhat oversimplified terms, the answer is by employing people to produce something not currently consumed. An excess of total income over total consumption can be provided in two principal ways:

1. by building up the total of plants and equipment and 2. by increasing the country's inventories of goods.

These two processes mean that people are putting their money into *things*, either directly via the purchase of bricks and machinery or indirectly by purchasing securities. The investing that offsets and permits the saving does not have to be done by the same persons who do the saving. The investing may be done either by the savers or by others. The "others" may include, for example, businessmen who borrow the savers' savings and spend the money for capital goods, businesses that borrow from banks to finance inventory increases, or corporations that use accumulated cash to build new plants.*

What prompts people to make such investments? People ordinarily make investments only when they have confidence that the ventures will turn out to be profitable. This confidence is often like a delicate flower, although it flourishes with weed-like vigor at infrequent intervals. If something happens to chill the enthusiasm of investors so that they reduce their investing in capital goods, how do the men who were employed in building plants, making machinery, and increasing inventories find work? The blunt and simple answer is that they don't.

Do they fail to find employment because the people who formerly saved and invested do not now wish to save and instead want to spend all their money on consumer goods? The answer to this question is a plain and definite "No." The people still want to save, but because they and other investors do not want to invest, they reduce their investing. Then something happens which illustrates the difference between *individual* business operations and *group* economic processes. If the would-be savers and the other investors reduce their investing, they throw people out of work or fail to provide work for others. The unemployed then

---

* It is important to note that just as some persons can save without investing, some persons can invest without saving—in one or more of the three ways mentioned above.

reduce their spending, and the upshot of the process is that the total income of the people of the country goes down. This reduction in general income reacts upon the would-be savers, and they presently find that their incomes have gone down and that the money which they hoped to save, but not invest, is no longer coming in. The result is, broadly speaking and for the people as a whole, but not—let it be emphasized—for every single individual, that the *total* of *actual saving* goes down just as fast as the *total* of *actual investing*. The two rates, indeed, are always equal.

This consequence results because the savers as a group are trying to do something which, under our present monetary system, is almost impossible of achievement. The savers are predominantly trying to *save* money without *investing* it. This means that the people as a whole are trying to accumulate more cash. But the people cannot accumulate more cash unless the total quantity of money is increased, and there is nothing in the present American monetary system to cause the total quantity of money to grow under these circumstances and during that precise period. This leads to the very natural conclusion that whenever the investors want to stop investing and start saving cash—if it were possible to switch the workmen who had been building plants and making new machinery to the *figurative making of new money*—we could accomplish the tricks of preserving employment, keeping the total of incomes up, and at the same time satisfying the desire of the public to save money without investing it. One of the purposes of the functional fiscal-monetary system that is described later is to accomplish these results.

THE PSYCHOLOGICAL FACTOR

In the psychological attitudes of people can be found an important partial explanation of the business cycle. Psychology is not a thing apart from the factors that have been discussed in the preceding sections. On the contrary, it is part and parcel of them. "Money," as Professor Carver once observed, "having no organs of locomotion, does not move of itself." * Money is received, spent, saved, and held by *human beings*. Decisions to save or to spend, to hold money or to invest it, depend on psychological factors. These, in turn, are affected by logic and by emotion and are influenced by ignorance and by knowledge.

So important indeed is the psychological condition that it is no exaggeration to say that if the people generally (or only the businessmen and investors) suddenly became convinced that there was going to be a serious depression, there probably would be one. For, if they were convinced, they would reduce their outlays, and such action would precipitate a depression.

The importance of taking account of psychological forces is immense in the planning of a stabilization program. The success of such a program depends to a very large extent on the confidence that the people have in it. If they believe that the stabilization program is a good one and will really work, the battle is more than half won. Shakespeare's observation that "There is nothing good or bad but thinking makes it so" applies with special force to stabilization programs.

THE MULTIPLE EFFECT OF CHANGES IN SPENDING†

If any unit—an individual, a business, or a governmental unit— increases its spending, a secondary increase is likely to follow.

* T. N. Carver, *Principles of National Economy* (Boston: Ginn & Co., 1921), p. 386.

† The term, "the multiple effect," is the same one that I used in my book, *Money, Business, and Prices* (London: P. S. King & Son, 1933). Students of monetary theory may wonder why I have not changed to using the term, "the multiplier"—which is now widely used. The reason is that the term, "the multiplier," is used by many writers as applying solely or especially to changes in *investment* outlays. I do not mean the term, "the multiple effect," to be restricted thus but rather to apply to any change of spending, whether investment outlays, wage payments, consumer expenditure, government outlays, or any other type.

Conversely, any decrease in spending is likely to cause a further decrease.

If the public increases its expenditures on consumer goods, then the retailers, wholesalers, and manufacturers are likely to increase their outlays. The recipients of the money which the public is increasingly spending are unlikely to try to hold on to all of it. Some of it will be re-spent by the recipients. Similarly, if investors increase their outlays on capital goods, this money is likely to be spent again by the people who receive it.

This fact helps to explain the reason for spending as it increases, to tend to keep on increasing, and as it declines, to tend to continue to decline. Suppose, for example, that businessmen reduce their expenditures on plant, equipment, or current production. Other businessmen, seeing their own sales volume and money receipts declining, are likely to restrict their outlays, also. Workers are likely to be discharged. They, in turn, will reduce their purchases. If this process gathers size and speed, the vicious downward spiral gets under way, and every reduction in spending stimulates a further contraction of business and employment. The reverse process occurs when spending is increasing.

THE PROBLEM OF STABILITY

A depression may be started by any one of a variety of causes—failure of a large bank (as in 1907), collapse of a speculative price level (1920), or a stock market break (1929). The initiating cause, however, is of minor importance when compared with the cumulative downward movement which ensues. This vicious circle is like the metaphorical snowball that goes down hill ever faster, gathering size as it goes. The real problem, therefore, is the means of preventing this cumulative downward movement—how to prevent a small business break from snowballing into a major depression.

To use another analogy, a person who knows how to ride a bicycle accomplishes an extraordinarily difficult feat—he continually recovers his balance; putting it another way, he continually corrects the ever-present tendency to fall, which is characteristic of the inherent instability of the combination of bicycle and rider. The performance is such a delicate one that a physicist friend tells me that any physicist who had never seen a man ride a bicycle would have no hesitation in stating that such a feat was impossible.

A person who does not know how to do the trick rides a shorter or longer distance, and he falls when his ability to cope with inherent instability becomes inadequate. Our economic system presents a picture much like that of the unskilled rider. The level of business is unstable, and it moves readily one way or the other.

The unskilled rider's trouble can be remedied in either of two major ways: 1. The bicycle can be converted into a tricycle by the addition of a third wheel and thus made inherently stable or 2. The rider can develop his skill and learn how to keep going in an upright position.

The program described in this book may be described as a combination, for the economic system, of the two methods. It aims at decreasing the natural instability of economic activity and also at developing a sort of national skill in keeping our economic machine in an upright condition. This should not be too difficult for a nation whose children can learn to ride bicycles.

SUMMARY

1. A highly developed economy cannot use barter; it must use money—a medium of exchange.

2. In a free society people are free to save money or to spend it.

3. If the desire to save outruns the willingness to invest, total spending declines.

4. If a decline in spending starts, it tends to spread, producing a multiple effect.

5. Stabilization of spending can be encouraged by methods calculated to reduce changes in spending and by invoking counteracting mechanisms that are designed to neutralize the variations in the public's desire to spend, thus arresting upward or downward spirals of self-feeding contraction or undue expansion.

CHAPTER 9

Money and Its Uses

INASMUCH AS *money*—ITS QUANTITY AND ITS USES—PLAYS SO VITAL A role in cyclical fluctuations, it is appropriate at this point to get clearly in mind certain key concepts about money and monetary processes. Armed with this understanding, we can then proceed to discuss the relationships among money, spending, prices, and production.

WHAT IS MONEY?

The experts disagree, to some extent, about the meaning of the word "money." There is, therefore, some disagreement about what *is* to be counted and what *is not* to be counted in calculating the total amount of money. In this book "money" means all the currency and bank deposits (demand and time) held by individuals, non-banking corporations, and governmental entities. It does not include the currency and bank deposits held by banks, except foreign banks. The total amount of money, thus defined, is the same as the figures given in the *Federal Reserve Bulletin* under the heading, "Total Deposits and Currency." On June 30, 1950 the nation's money supply included the following items.

TABLE 13.   THE AMOUNT OF MONEY IN THE
UNITED STATES AS OF JUNE 30, 1950

Location	Millions
Currency outside banks	$ 25,185
Time deposits	59,739
Demand deposits	85,040
U.S. Government balances	
At Federal Reserve banks	950
At commercial and savings banks	3,801
Treasury cash	1,298
Foreign bank deposits	2,555
Total	$178,568

Source: *Federal Reserve Bulletin,* June 1953, p. 614.

Some analysts consider that time deposits should not be classified as "money." The reasons seem to be that time deposits do not circulate and that before time deposits can be spent they must be exchanged for currency or for demand deposits. Is this, however, an adequate reason for not counting them as money? Let us examine the matter.

Time deposits consist of dollars. They do not consist of securities. They are classified on any balance sheet, together with currency and demand deposits, as "Cash." If a newly created dollar could be followed as it moves from hand to hand, it would be found—at any moment in one of these three places—demand deposits, time deposits, or currency. It hardly seems reasonable to say that a dollar is money as long as it is held as currency, continues to be money when deposited in a demand bank account, but ceases to be money if it rests in a time or savings account.

"MONEY IN CIRCULATION"

The term, "money in circulation," is used in several different ways. Sometimes it refers to the currency outside banks—in the hands of the general public. Sometimes it is used in an attempt to distinguish between those bank deposits which are in circulation and those which are not. In whichever of these ways the phrase is used, however, it is misleading, if not actually completely wrong.

Every dollar, both of currency and bank deposits, is at every moment part of someone's money stock. None is "in circulation" in the sense of being in passage from one money stock to another. When a money payment is made, the dollars jump from one person's money stock to another's.

There is, to be sure, an important phenomenon which is called the "circulation of money." But the circulation occurs instantaneously, and there is no money *actually* in circulation.

A physical analogy may be helpful. Water circulates through the pipes of a municipal water system. The quantity in the pipes is measurable and might be described as "water in circulation." Frequent usage of the term "money in circulation" suggests a similar body of money in motion. A better analogy, however, would be that of the circulation of electricity. Electricity circulates, but its movement is (virtually) instantaneous. One would not speak of "the amount of electricity in circulation." So it is with money. It circulates, but there is none actually circulating.

DEMAND AND TIME DEPOSITS

The foregoing discussion may seem to be mere hair-splitting, but it is not. Its significance flows from the attempts made to distinguish between types of money which do and do not circulate, or which are or are not in circulation.

Specifically, demand deposits (checking accounts) are sometimes held to be money which circulates, and time deposits (saving accounts) are described either as money which does not circulate or as not money at all.

Actually, it is not possible to identify particular dollars as cir-

culating or not circulating. One or two simple examples will
make the point clear. Assume that a man keeps his dollars in the
form of currency and that he has several thousand dollars in a
chest in his home. Are these dollars in circulation? None is actually
in circulation. Some occasionally come into the chest; others leave
it. Is it possible to distinguish among the various dollars in the
chest, saying that some circulate and others do not? Some of the
dollars, to be sure, may have lain at the bottom of the chest for
years. But is any useful purpose served by distinguishing them
from the others? Would the significant facts be altered if the man
followed the steady practice of putting newly arrived dollars at
one end of the chest and taking out dollars from the other end?
All would eventually go out. But would they be "circulating" in
any more significant sense than before?

Now suppose that the man, deciding it is unsafe to keep so
many dollars in his house, opens a checking account. If he continues to use currency, and lets the checking account lie idle,
shall it be said that the checking account dollars are not circulating? Or, alternatively, if he uses the checking account and leaves
the chest alone, is it correct to say the currency is out of circulation? If he were to open a savings account, these same questions
could properly be repeated.

The conclusions of this analysis are these:

1. There is no money actually in circulation.

2. The circulation of money, however, is a very real phenomenon.

3. There is no logical basis for distinguishing between dollars
which circulate and those which do not.

4. No useful purpose is served by trying to make such a distinction; on the contrary, it is confusing.

5. All forms of money—currency, demand deposits, and time
deposits—are equally part of someone's money stock and not in
circulation; it is unsound to distinguish among them on the
ground that some circulate and others do not.

SAVING, BANK LOANS, AND INVESTMENT

In the preceding chapter, it was argued that some of the population cannot save money unless others are either dis-saving or investing. It may be asked, "If the savers save money and put it in the bank, do not the bank's deposits increase, and cannot the bank turn around and lend the money?" In terms of a single bank, the answer is "Yes." But for *the entire banking system,* the answer is "No." The money that a given depositor has saved comes from other persons whose bank deposits are reduced as his rises. The favorable clearing house balance that his bank experiences is offset by the unfavorable balances imposed on other banks. The banks as a whole have no more deposits than before, and they have therefore no additional lending capacity.

Indeed, the ability of the banking system to increase the amount of its loans is not affected by depositors saving and being thrifty or spending their money wildly. Neither line of action changes the total of deposits.

The condition that does determine the ability of the banks to lend more is the state of their reserves. If they hold more cash reserves than required by law, custom, or prudence, they can increase their loans and investments—if they wish to do so. If they do not have such "excess reserves," they cannot. The saving and spending behavior of their depositors does not affect the amount of their excess reserves. The quantity of excess reserves is influenced by: 1. gold flows, 2. the actions of the Federal Reserve System, and 3. the banks themselves, in increasing or decreasing their loans and investments—and, thereby, their deposits.

If people wish to save money, one way of providing the offsetting investment that will enable them to do so is for the banks to expand their assets. But this depends on their possessing or acquiring excess reserves, not on the actions of the savers.

THE CIRCULAR FLOW OF MONEY

The level of cyclical prosperity may be pictured as consisting of two great flows—one of money and the other of goods and services. In this simplified picture, the families of the country are seen to consist of consumers and workers. The workers sell their work to businesses and are paid in money. The families buy the goods produced by the businesses, paying for them with the money received as wages. Businesses pay out the money—as wages. Thus the money is seen to go around and around—a process sometimes described as the "circular flow of money."

This simplified picture is illustrated in the accompanying diagram, Chart 2. Note that the diagram does not include *government*, an omission made for the sake of simplicity.

CHART 2. THE CIRCULAR FLOW OF MONEY, GOODS, AND WORK

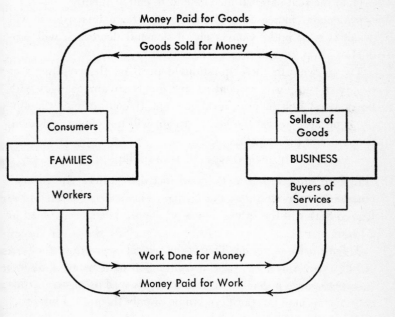

When the money flows more rapidly, the increase may be described in three ways:

1. Effective demand has increased;
2. Spending has increased; and
3. The national income, in dollars, has increased.

The reverse of these three statements is true when the money flows more slowly instead of more rapidly.

Note that the third statement relates to the *money* national income, not necessarily to the *real* national income, which is the flow labeled "Goods" in the diagram.

THE RELATIONSHIPS BETWEEN DEMAND, PRICES, AND PRODUCTION

Since the real national income is the important thing, let us ask, "When the money flows more rapidly or more slowly, what happens to the real national income and to employment?"

If demand increases, will the goods stream increase, or will prices rise, or both? Conversely, if demand decreases, will production drop, or will prices fall, or both?

The answers to these questions depend on the conditions of *supply*. If supply is *responsive*, the goods stream changes with the demand, but the price level does not. If, contrariwise, the supply is nonresponsive, the goods stream will not change with the demand, but prices will.

There are six principal types of relationship.

1. Pure price inflation. Demand increases; prices rise proportionately; production does not change. This will not occur in the United States in the future unless we should become involved in a major war.

2. Pure price deflation. This is the logical opposite of the preceding type. Since, however, a contraction of demand is almost certain to cause a decline in production as well as in prices, this relationship may be considered to be of only theoretical interest.

3. *Mixed inflation.* Demand increases; both prices and production rise. This is likely to occur when a nation is recovering from a depression.

4. *Mixed deflation.* Demand decreases; both prices and production decline. This is likely to happen as a nation enters a depression.

5. *Pure production expansion.* Demand increases; production rises proportionately; prices do not change. This pattern would characterize an expanding economy—one in which national productive capacity is increasing.

6. *Pure production contraction.* Demand decreases; production contracts proportionately; prices remain unchanged. This, similarly to pure price deflation, is unlikely, because a contraction in demand is almost certain to cause both prices and production to decline.

Three of these six combinations are unlikely to occur in the United States 1. pure price inflation, 2. pure price deflation, and 6. pure production contraction.

Two of the others comprise the typical "business cycle." They are: 3. mixed inflation and 4. mixed deflation. Their prevention is a national objective.

The remaining one—5. pure production expansion—is a proper national objective. Since these three are of concern to us, they are illustrated in Chart 3.

There are thus seen to be two interrelated problems concerning the flow of money (demand, spending, and the money national income). One is that of avoiding short-run ups and downs. The other is that of achieving a gradual growth, in the long run, at an appropriate rate.

The relationships described in this section, to be examined in greater detail in the next two chapters, may be expressed by some simple equations. These formulas will be useful in connection with the analysis in the next section.

CHART 3. HOW CHANGES IN DEMAND AFFECT
PRODUCTION AND PRICES

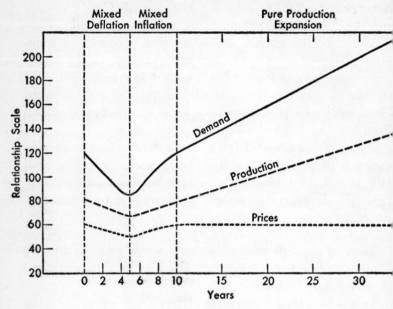

Let

$$I = \text{the national income, in money}$$

Let

$$G = \text{goods, or the } \textit{real} \text{ national income}$$

Let

$$P = \text{the average price of the goods that comprise the real national income}$$

Then

$$1. \quad I = PG \, *$$

and

$$2. \quad \frac{I}{G} = P$$

* Strictly speaking, this should read $I = \Sigma pg$, but the expression given above is suggestive enough for present purposes.

Because of the importance of the flow of money, it is desirable to analyze some essential interrelationships between the *flow* of money and the *amount* of money. To this analysis we now turn attention.

THE RELATIONSHIPS BETWEEN THE FLOW
OF MONEY AND THE AMOUNT OF MONEY

The total flow of money may increase or decrease, unaccompanied by any change in the amount of money. That is, the average dollar may change hands more rapidly or more slowly. This aspect of the relationship between demand for and the amount of money is called "velocity of circulation of money." Attention is being focused here on what is called *income* velocity of circulation. This is the ratio between 1. national income and 2. the amount of money.

The relations of velocity to the equations introduced in the preceding section are these:

Let

$$V = \text{velocity}$$

Then

$$M = \text{money}$$

$$3. \quad V = \frac{I}{M}$$

and

$$4. \quad I = MV$$

Since

$$I = PG \qquad \text{(Equation 1)}$$

and

$$I = MV \qquad \text{(Equation 4)}$$

we may write:

$$5. \quad MV = PG$$

Students of economics will note that this equation is almost identical to an old friend: $MV = PT$. The obvious difference is in the last letter, and this difference changes the value for P and V. The value T includes *all* transactions for which money payments are made—for instance, payments for farm labor, wheat, flour, and bread. The value G includes only the bread—symbolic of the final goods that comprise the national income. Since G is only a small part of T, the total value of each side of Equation 5 is much smaller, the value of V correspondingly smaller, and the value of P presumably different.

Velocity is, by definition, a mathematical relationship. But it is more than a figure computed from two other figures. It measures the average desires of people to use their money, to get rid of cash, to buy—consumer goods, producer goods, stocks, bonds, or something else. In short, a rise or fall in velocity is an index of the various psychological factors that cause people to decide to use their money.

Some conditions that might cause people to use their money faster are these:

1. An expectation that prices will rise
2. An expectation that business will improve and profits will increase
3. An expectation that employment and incomes will go up

Opposite expectations—that these various items will drop—would be likely to cause people to be less desirous of using their money.

The changes that occurred in velocity during the great business fluctuations between 1929 and 1948 are shown in Table 14.

It is clear, therefore, that changes in the velocity of circulation of money constitute an important force in the business cycle. Indeed, the problem of cyclical stability may be described as the problem of stabilizing MV. The long-run problem in an expanding

TABLE 14. MONEY, NATIONAL INCOME, AND
VELOCITY OF CIRCULATION, 1929–1948

Year	Amount of Money (Billions)	National Income (Billions)	Ratio of National Income to Money (V)
1929	$ 55.8	$ 87.4	1.57
1930	55.2	75.0	1.36
1931	53.7	58.9	1.10
1932	45.7	41.7	.91
1933	42.0	39.6	.94
1934	49.0	48.6	.99
1935	53.1	56.8	1.07
1936	58.7	64.7	1.10
1937	61.5	73.6	1.20
1938	60.0	67.4	1.12
1939	65.4	72.5	1.11
1940	70.7	81.3	1.15
1941	79.4	103.8	1.31
1942	86.1	137.1	1.59
1943	114.8	169.7	1.48
1944	141.6	183.8	1.30
1945	168.0	182.7	1.09
1946	176.2	180.3	1.02
1947	169.2	198.7	1.17
1948	172.9	223.5	1.29

SOURCE: Money and national income figures, see Table 15, footnotes 4 and 7,
p. 133.

economy may be described as increasing MV at an appropriate
rate, through the years and the decades.

Before turning attention to methods of solving these problems,
let us examine another basic relationship between money and demand—one which is perhaps less well understood than is the concept of velocity.

THE DEMAND FOR MONEY

As noted earlier in this chapter, all money belongs to someon Every dollar is always part of someone's money stock. On June 3C 1950 our people (individuals, corporations, governments, etc. held $178,568,000,000 in cash—currency and bank deposits. Thi was not in stocks, bonds, buildings, machinery, or inventories— not in *things*, but it was *money*.

This money may well be described by Mr. Hawtrey's term, "th unspent margin." * For the most part such money earns no inter est. A perfectly fair question, therefore, would be: "Why d people hold so much cash?"

There are several answers:

1. To bridge the gap between income and expenditures
2. To do business, as in making change in stores
3. While accumulating money to buy something
4. In expectation of being able to buy things at lower prices later on
5. To guard against contingencies and emergencies
6. To feel secure

Whatever the reasons, it is clear that people do desire to have stock of money. If they did not have this desire, they could easil get rid of their money. That is, any individual could do so. Since however, his action in using his money merely shifts the money to someone else, the total of money would not thereby be reduced What would happen, therefore, if people generally decided to hold less money? If they generally increased their money outlays the total money flow would increase, and (among other increases) the money national income would rise. These actions would no reduce the total amount of money, but they would reduce the ratio of money to national income.

* R. G. Hawtrey, *The Art of Central Banking* (New York: Longmans Green & Co., Inc., 1932), p. 106.

This ratio may be taken to represent the *demand for money.* Note that this term does not mean what it commonly means in financial circles. There it means the desire to *borrow* money. The term as used here, however, means the demonstrated desire to have a quantity of cash.

This concept may now be related to those discussed above and to the simple equations. (Students of monetary theory may be interested in the footnote.) *

Let D = the demand for money,
     (expressed as a fraction of national income)

Then

$$6. \quad D = \frac{M}{I}$$

and

$$7. \quad I = \frac{M}{D}$$

$$8. \quad M = DI$$

These concepts may be illustrated by using the appropriate figures for the year 1950. The average amount of money was about $180 billion. The national income was just over $240 billion. Equation 6 expresses the demand for money as

$$D = \frac{M}{I}, \text{ or } \frac{\$180 \text{ billion}}{\$240 \text{ billion}} = 0.75$$

That is to say, in that year people were desirous of holding a total amount of money equal to 0.75 (or 75 per cent) of their total incomes.

* Equation 8 resembles the equation $M = kY$, which is often associated with the name of Alfred Marshall. The symbol k carries the connotation that the value is a constant. Since, however, the demand for money is not a constant, the symbol k is misleading.

EFFECTS OF CHANGES IN THE DEMAND FOR MONEY

Equation 7 is especially important because it sheds light
the means by which the size of the money national income (a
demand and spending) are determined. Equation 7, $I = M/D$,
1950 was in dollars, $240 billion = $180 billion/0.75. Recalli
what was said a few paragraphs back, we may ask, "What wou
happen to the national income if the demand for money were
rise or to fall?" Suppose that it were to fall from 0.75 to 0.6
People would be trying to unload cash—necessarily onto someo
else. Since, however, most of the "someone else's" are trying to
the same thing, velocity of circulation would increase, and t
national income would rise to $300 billion. The amount of mon
would not have declined, but people would hold an amount
cash equal to only 60 per cent of their incomes, instead of t
previous 75 per cent. The equation reads: $300 billion = $18
billion/0.60.

If, conversely, the demand for money were to rise (say to 0.90
velocity would decrease as would the national income—to $2
billion. The values in the the equation would be: $200 billion
$180 billion/0.90.

The foregoing analysis illustrates the ways in which money flov
are determined—why the money national income, demand, ar
spending increase or decrease, in response to changes in the d
mand for money.

If the demand for money never changed, this discussion of t
public's desire to hold cash would be of little importance. In fac
however, the demand for money is not steady and unchangin
Since the year 1800 (as will be shown in detail in the next cha
ter), it has risen greatly.

In 1800, the value of D was 0.056. That is, the amount of mone
was 5.6 per cent of the national income. In 1850, the value of .
had risen to 0.161, in 1900 to 0.549, and in 1950 to 0.747.

The value of D also has displayed a cyclical fluctuation. In 192 t stood at 0.65 ($55.8 billion divided by $87.4 billion). It rose to .06 in 1933 and stood at 0.77 in 1941.

Mathematically, V and D are reciprocals. If, for instance, one were to double, the other would be halved. This fact may suggest that they are merely different symbols for the same thing. But not so. They are interrelated, but as symbols they stand for different bundles of psychological attitudes and decisions.

Since Equation 7 says $I = M/D$, we may restate the two central problems as follows:

1. The business cycle problem calls for stabilizing M/D.

2. The long-run problem requires an increase in M/D, at appropriate rates.

THE BARE BONES OF THE PROBLEMS

The *long-run* problem of accommodating and stimulating the economic growth of the United States requires a suitable increase in the flow of money. This may be described as achieving gradual rises in MV and in M/D. Throughout much of American history, V has declined; D has risen; and M has grown faster than the real national income. The reasons for these changes and their significance for the future of American prosperity will be discussed in the following chapters.

The *short-run* problem—the business cycle—may be described as the problem of stabilizing MV or M/D. In the past, each of the three components has tended to vary in a *cycle-intensifying manner*. That is, when business is declining, M and V go down, and D goes up.

Hence the solution of the problem of preventing depressions has three facets, which may be combined:

1. Preventing a drop in M and, instead, causing M to increase
2. Restraining a decline in V
3. Restraining a rise in D

A further question is this: How can these things be done with a minimum of intervention by the government? The answer to this question depends on another question: How much can the private sectors of the economy do toward achieving these aims? The more the private sectors can do, the less will remain for the government to do. Attention will be given to the things that the private sectors can do and what the government should do in the chapters immediately following.

SUMMARY

Here are the chief points made in this chapter:

1. Money includes currency outside banks and bank deposits—demand and time.

2. Every dollar always belongs to someone. None is ever "in circulation."

3. Money circulates, however, by jumping from one person's money stock to another. This circulation may be described as the flow of money, as effective demand, or (a portion of it) as the money national income.

4. The ratio of the national income to the quantity of money measures its velocity of circulation.

5. The desire to hold money may be measured by the proportion of national income represented by the quantity of money.

6. The short-run problem—stabilizing the aggregate money flow—requires proper behavior of: a. velocity of circulation, b. the demand for money, and c. the quantity of money.

7. The long-run problem, in an expanding economy like ours, necessitates appropriate gradual changes in these same three factors—in order to provide an expanding demand to accommodate increasing productive capacity.

CHAPTER 10

Money, Spending, and Prices

THAT THERE IS A RELATIONSHIP BETWEEN THE AMOUNT OF MONEY, the rate of spending, and the general level of prices is a very old proposition in economic analysis. A common formulation of the relationship is the one that is called the "quantity theory." It is usually stated thus: Other things being equal, a change in the quantity of money will be accompanied by a proportionate change in the general level of prices. Stated in this way, it is true. The qualifying phrase, "other things being equal," preserves its validity. Much of the writing on this subject has apparently assumed that the "other things" did *in fact* remain equal. The "other things" are these: the quantity of goods, the velocity of circulation of money, and the demand for money. If these things are assumed to be unchanged, one is in effect talking about a *stationary state*. Much of the printed analysis (in bygone years, at least) of the relationship between the quantity of money and the price level has apparently proceeded on these assumptions. In the terms suggested in the preceding chapter, the monetary changes result only in either pure price inflation or in pure price deflation.

When the other things are not assumed to be equal, however and when the analysis relates not to a stationary state but to a expanding economy, the quantity theory must be modified accordingly.

These modifications are strikingly illustrated by the historica experience of the United States. Study of this experience indicate that the simple quantity theory is inapplicable to this country. Th supply of money has grown rapidly, but except during wartime the price level has usually declined.

MONEY AND PRICES IN AN EXPANDING ECONOMY

Many of the key figures in the economic history of the Unite States have been brought together in Table 15 and illustrated graphically in Chart 4. Indeed, the table and chart together con stitute a kind of compressed summary of the economic history o our country. They show the growth of the money supply, the in crease of population, the rise of national income and nationa wealth, and the ups and downs of the price level. Frequent refer ence will be made to this table and the chart. The reader wil find the facts portrayed in them both vital in themselves and basi to the analysis of prosperity.

A NOTE ON THE CHART

Readers who are acquainted with types of graph papers and graph grids will have instantly recognized Chart 4 as being a semilogarithmic or ratio chart. For other readers a word of ex planation may be helpful.

This chart uses a type of grid in which an increase in magni tude at a constant geometric rate (for example, 100 per cent every ten years) appears as a straight line. The reader can test this readily by taking such a series—2, 4, 8, 16, 32, 64, 128—and plot-

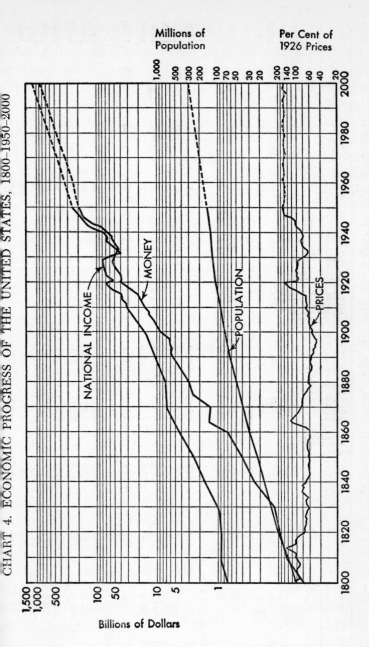

CHART 4. ECONOMIC PROGRESS OF THE UNITED STATES, 1800–1950–2000

Millions of
Population

Per Cent of
1926 Prices

Billions of Dollars

NATIONAL INCOME

MONEY

POPULATION

PRICES

TABLE 15. ECONOMIC PROGRESS OF THE UNITED STATES, 1800–1950

Year	Population (Millions)	Money in Circulation (Millions)	Bank Deposits (Millions)	Total Money (Millions)	Wholesale Prices (1926 = 100)	National Wealth (Billions)	National Income (Billions)	Money per Capita	Wealth per Capita	Income per Capita	Year
Decennial Figures											
1800	5.3	$ 27	$ 11	$ 38	101.6	$ 0.6	$ 0.7	$ 7	$ 113	$ 131	1800
1810	7.2	55	22	77	107.7	1.2	0.9	10	167	130	1810
1820	9.6	67	27	94	76.6	2.6	0.9	10	271	93	1820
1830	12.9	87	35	122	65.6	3.8	1.0	9	297	78	1830
1840	17.1	186	76	262	71.1	5.2	1.6	15	304	98	1840
1850	23.3	279	110	389	62.3	7.1	2.4	17	305	107	1850
1860	31.5	435	254	689	60.9	16.2	4.3	22	514	140	1860
Quinquennial Figures											
1865	35.7	1,084	458	1,542	132.0			43			1865
1870	39.9	775	598	1,373	86.7	30.1	6.8	34	754	173	1870
1875	45.1	834	1,787	2,621	77.7			58			1875
1880	50.3	973	1,952	2,925	65.1	43.6	7.2	58	867	147	1880
1885	56.7	1,293	2,734	4,027	56.6			71			1885
1890	63.1	1,429	4,074	5,503	56.2	65.0	10.7	87	1,030	173	1890
Annual Figures											
1892	65.7	1,015	4,823	5,838	52.2			89			1892
1893	67.0	1,081	4,787	5,868	53.4			88			1893
1894	68.3	972	4,815	5,787	47.9			85			1894
1895	69.6	971	5,061	6,032	48.8			87			1895
1896	70.9	974	5,074	6,048	46.5			85			1896
1897	72.2	1,013	5,192	6,205	46.6			86			1897
1898	73.5	1,150	5,882	7,032	48.5		15.4	96			1898
1899	74.8	1,181	6,855	8,036	52.2			107		205	1899

130

Year											Year
1900	212	1,163	116	16.2	88.5	56.1	8,865	7,534	1,331	76.1	1900
1901			129			55.5	10,013	8,618	1,395	77.6	1901
1902			137			58.9	10,839	9,408	1,431	79.2	1902
1903		1,303	142			59.6	11,452	9,909	1,543	80.6	1903
1904			146		107.1	59.7	11,973	10,411	1,562	82.2	1904
1905			158			60.1	13,237	11,608	1,629	83.8	1905
1906			165			61.8	14,121	12,362	1,759	85.4	1906
1907			174			65.2	15,102	13,402	1,700	87.0	1907
1908			166			62.9	14,718	13,007	1,711	88.7	1908
1909			175			67.6	15,794	14,103	1,691	90.5	1909
1910	358		184	33.1		70.4	16,977	15,252	1,725	92.4	1910
1911	346		189	32.5	186.3	64.9	17,762	16,053	1,709	93.9	1911
1912	362		198	34.5		69.1	18,865	17,103	1,762	95.3	1912
1913	389		200	37.8		69.8	19,403	17,545	1,858	97.2	1913
1914	367		202	36.4		68.1	20,031	18,498	1,533	99.1	1914
1915	381		206	38.3		69.5	20,682	19,107	1,575	100.5	1915
1916	440		238	44.9		85.5	24,302	22,426	1,876	102.0	1916
1917	517		275	53.4		117.5	28,422	26,146	2,276	103.3	1917
1918	563		305	58.1		131.3	31,489	28,191	3,298	103.2	1918
1919	633		341	66.1		138.6	35,656	32,063	3,593	104.5	1919
1920	655		374	73.4		154.4	39,884	35,779	4,105	106.5	1920
1921	487		349	58.3		97.6	37,834	34,157	3,677	108.5	1921
1922	550	2,914	354	60.5	320.8	96.7	39,031	35,685	3,346	110.1	1922
1923	626		382	70.7		100.6	42,780	39,041	3,739	111.9	1923
1924	614		390	70.6		98.1	44,553	40,903	3,650	114.1	1924
1925	646		418	75.2		103.5	48,348	44,775	3,573	115.8	1925
1926	655		431	80.4		100.0	50,581	46,980	3,601	117.4	1926
1927	642		439	78.5		95.4	52,260	48,704	3,556	119.0	1927
1928	666		454	81.0		96.7	54,702	51,056	3,622	120.5	1928
1929	717		458	87.4		95.3	55,776	52,137	3,639	121.8	1929

Year	Population (Millions)	Money in Circulation (Millions)	Bank Deposits (Millions)	Total Money (Millions)	Wholesale Prices (1926 = 100)	National Wealth (Billions)	National Income (Billions)	Money per Capita	Wealth per Capita	Income per Capita	Year
1930	123.1	3,369	51,859	55,228	86.4	428.1	75.0	449	3,478	610	1930
1931	124.0	3,651	50,034	53,685	73.0		58.9	433		475	1931
1932	124.8	4,616	41,104	45,720	64.8		41.7	366		326	1932
1933	125.6	4,761	37,268	42,029	65.9		39.6	335		315	1933
1934	126.4	4,659	44,341	49,000	74.9		48.6	388		384	1934
1935	127.3	4,783	48,296	53,079	80.0		56.8	417		445	1935
1936	128.1	5,222	53,490	58,712	80.8		64.7	458		505	1936
1937	128.8	5,489	56,038	61,527	86.3		73.6	478		571	1937
1938	129.8	5,417	54,612	60,029	78.6	388.4	67.4	462	2,992	520	1938
1939	130.9	6,005	59,436	65,441	77.1		72.5	500		554	1939
1940	132.0	6,699	64,048	70,747	78.6		81.3	536		616	1940
1941	133.2	8,204	71,153	79,357	87.3		103.8	596		780	1941
1942	134.7	10,936	75,128	86,064	98.8		137.1	639		1,018	1942
1943	136.5	15,814	98,998	114,812	103.1		169.7	841		1,243	1943
1944	138.1	20,881	120,670	141,551	104.0		183.8	1,025		1,331	1944
1945	139.6	25,097	142,943	168,040	105.8		182.7	1,204		1,309	1945
1946	141.2	26,516	149,699	176,215	121.1		180.3	1,248		1,277	1946
1947	144.0	26,299	142,935	169,234	152.1		198.7	1,175		1,380	1947
1948	146.6	25,638	147,219	172,857	165.1		213.5	1,179		1,525	1948
1949	149.2	25,266	146,336	171,602	155.0		216.3	1,150		1,449	1949
1950	151.7	25,185	153,383	178,568	161.5		240.6	1,177		1,585	1950

SOURCES: See p. 133.

SOURCES:

1. Of population: 1800–1945, U.S. Bureau of the Census, *Historical Statistics of the United States* (Washington: U.S. Government Printing Office, 1949), p. 26; since 1945, Bureau of the Census' estimates for July 1.

2. Of money in circulation: 1800–1890, *Historical Statistics of the United States*, p. 274; 1892–1940, Federal Reserve Board, *Banking and Monetary Statistics* (Washington: National Capitol Press, 1943), pp. 34, 35; since 1940, *Federal Reserve Bulletin*.

3. Of bank deposits: 1840–1890, U.S. Bureau of the Census, *Statistical Abstract of the United States* (Washington: U.S. Government Printing Office, 1942), p. 291; 1892–1915, *Banking and Monetary Statistics*, p. 34: since 1915, *Federal Reserve Bulletin* and Federal Reserve mimeographed tables. The figures for 1800 to 1830 are estimated by the present writer and are based on the ratios between deposits and circulation in 1840 and 1850.

4. Of total money: totals of the two immediately preceding columns. The current figure is reported each month in the *Federal Reserve Bulletin* under the heading, "Deposits and Currency: Total."

5. Of wholesale prices: 1800, U.S. Bureau of Labor Statistics, *Bulletin No. 543, Wholesale Prices 1930*, p. 39; 1801–1945, *Historical Statistics of the United States*, pp. 232, 233; since 1945, *Federal Reserve Bulletin*.

6. Of national wealth: 1830–1922, *Historical Statistics of the United States*, pp. 9, 10; 1800–1820, 1930, 1938, Robert R. Doane, *The Anatomy of American Wealth* (New York: Harper & Bros., 1940), p. 26.

7. Of national income: 1800–1900 (actually [decennially] 1799–1899), from Robert F. Martin, *National Income in the United States, 1799–1938* (New York: National Industrial Conference Board, 1939), p. 6. It is the present writer's opinion that the figures for 1799 to 1819 are too high—by at least 100 per cent in 1799. The figures from 1910 through 1928 are those of the U.S. Department of Agriculture, *Net Farm Income and National Income Parity Summary, 1910–41* (Washington: U.S. Bureau of Agricultural Economics, 1942); since 1929, U.S. Department of Commerce, *National Income and Product, 1929–1950* (Washington: U.S. Government Printing Office, 1951), p. 150.

8. Of money per capita, wealth per capita, and income per capita: results of dividing total money, national wealth, and national income, respectively, by the population for the corresponding year.

Note: Many of the figures for the early years of this 150-year period are subject to a wide margin of error.

133

ting it on the chart. The resulting curve will be a straight line showing a constant geometric rate of increase.

This type of chart is useful, therefore, in testing such rates of change. It is also useful in comparing the geometric rates of change of two quantities. Finally, in this case, the increases in three of the items (national wealth, national income, and the amount of money) are so great that if they were shown on the more usual type of arithmetic grid, the curves would hug the bottom of the chart during the first decades of the period.

As Chart 4 shows, the rates of increase of population, wealth, income, and money were steady (remarkably steady, it might be said) from 1800 to 1929. Then the rate of increase of the population, which had been slowing down, dropped still more. The other three rates—money, income, and wealth—not only stopped increasing but began to decline. These decreases were not, moreover, the comparatively short, mild declines which had occurred before from time to time. On the contrary, they were so large and so prolonged that they looked like a reversal of the long-time growth trends.

The curves turned up in 1933 and rose rapidly during World War II and thereafter. In 1950 the nation's total production and the real national income were about one and three-fourths as great as in 1929.

MONEY AND PRICES IN A 150-YEAR PERIOD

The story told by the figures is clear. In 1940, the quantity of money in this country was 1,862 times as great as in 1800, but the wholesale price index was actually *lower*. The 1940 amount of money was eight times as great as the 1900 figure, and prices were only 40 per cent higher.

By 1950, however, because of inflationary war financing, the picture had changed substantially. The quantity of money had risen by 150 per cent since 1940, and prices had risen by 104 per cent. Prices in 1950 were 59 per cent higher than in 1800, and the amount of money was 4,699 times as large.

It is possible that the prices of many important commodities have declined and that these commodities are not included in the wholesale price index. Therefore, the rise in prices may be less than the index shows. The explanation of this proposition is a fourfold one:

1. Many important commodities (especially manufactured goods) are not included in the price indexes because they are not "standardized," i.e., their quality, content, or specifications change from time to time. Examples are radio sets, washing machines, and automobiles.

2. The typical price behavior of such goods is that their prices gradually decline as production techniques are improved and quantity output is achieved.

3. Coincidentally, there is typically an improvement in quality which is substantially equivalent to a reduction in price. Automobile tires are an example. They cost, in 1940, one-fourth of what they had twenty-five years before and in 1940 ran four times as far as in 1915. That is really the equivalent of a reduction of the price to one-sixteenth of the original price!

4. Brand-new products are developed that never existed before. George Washington, rich man and President, could not have purchased an automobile even if he had offered his entire fortune!

Four sharp upward swings in prices occurred—all in connection with wars. During peacetime prices usually drifted slowly downward, and the supply of money usually did not increase rapidly enough to prevent a price decline. During the four wars, however, the quantity of money increased so rapidly that the price level rose substantially.

In short, the 150-year period witnessed a tremendous increase in the money supply, while prices alternately rose and fell; at the end of the period (but not in 1940) the price index was substantially higher than in 1800. At no time, however, did prices rise as rapidly as did the supply of money.

This tremendous disparity between the 150-year growth in the quantity of money and the relatively slight increase in the price level calls for explanation. It is this: The United States was an *expanding* economy. The population was growing, and potential per capita production increased rapidly. These two variables are multiplicative and, together with the greater wealth and income that they create, explain why an expanding economy needs more money and can absorb substantial amounts of additional money without price inflation.

The relation of these key factors—population, wealth, and income—to money and prices is entitled to some further consideration.

POPULATION AND MONEY

One explanation of the disparity between the change in the country's money supply and the level of prices is the increase in the population. The population of the United States rose from 5.3 million in 1800 to 151.7 million in 1950. Hence, in 1950 there were some 29 times as many trouser pockets that needed some money. When there are more people who want to use and hold money, a proportionate increase in the total amount of money is not incompatible with a stationary commodity price level.

Actually, since the total amount of money increased much faster than the population, the per capita amount of money rose markedly. The amount of money per capita was $7 in 1800, $17 in 1850, $116 in 1900, and $1,177 in 1950. Despite this great increase in money per capita, the great gains in national income and wealth (and per capita income and wealth) very nearly offset the inflationary effect.

WEALTH AND MONEY

A second factor that helps to explain why prices have risen so much less than has the quantity of money is the immense growth in the national wealth of the United States. Table 16 brings together these figures and shows that the amount of money has grown faster than the national wealth, so that the percentage of money to the national wealth has grown fairly steadily.

TABLE 16. THE QUANTITY OF MONEY COMPARED
WITH THE NATIONAL WEALTH, 1800–1938

YEAR	MONEY	NATIONAL WEALTH	MONEY AS A FRACTION OF NATIONAL WEALTH
	(Millions)	*(Millions)*	
1800	$ 38	$ 620	0.061
1810	77	1,217	063
1820	94	2,588	036
1830	122	3,825	032
1840	262	5,226	050
1850	389	7,136	055
1860	689	16,160	043
1870	1,373	30,069	046
1880	2,925	43,642	067
1890	5,503	65,037	084
1900	8,865	88,517	100
1904	11,973	107,104	112
1912	18,865	186,300	101
1922	38,998	320,804	122
1930	54,389	428,126	127
1938	56,565	388,421	0.146

SOURCE: See Table 15, footnotes 4 and 6, p. 133.

Per capita wealth increased from $113 in 1800 to $2,992 in 1938. These figures show a development that is entirely reasonable, namely, that as people get richer they are disposed to hold an increasing amount of cash. They have bigger and better houses, better and more clothing, more automobiles, more investments, and are quite willing to save and hold more money, also.

The figures also show that there has been a gradual tendency for money to become a slightly larger fraction of the total national wealth than earlier. Is this not reasonable? As people get richer they can better afford to have some of their wealth in the form of money. At the same time, there has developed a decreasing use of *barter* and an increasing use of money as a method of exchanging goods. If, then, we wish to look forward to a continually rising national wealth in future decades, it is reasonable to expect that the total amount of money should increase at least as rapidly.

NATIONAL INCOME AND MONEY

Another reason why commodity prices have risen only slightly through the 150-year period, despite the great increase in the quantity of money, is the immense growth of the real national income (called G in Chapter 9). In 1799 the annual national income was $1.1 billion (converted to dollars having the purchasing power of those of 1950) or $206 per person. In 1950 the national income had risen to $240.6 billion, or $1,585 per capita. The basic causes of this increase were the rise in per capita output, which was discussed in Chapter 6, and the growth of the population, itself.

These increases in production and income have had a twofold impact on the need for, desire for, and ability to hold money. In the first place, the stream of goods (G) has risen greatly. This means that unless monetary velocity (V) rises, more money is continuously needed in order to buy the goods at a given level of prices. In the second place, as people's incomes rise, their money position becomes less "hand-to-mouth"—therefore, they can afford to hold more cash, no longer needing to spend their few dollars as

fast as they are reecived. Many people feel more comfortable with
larger cash balances. Hence the demand for money (*D*) rises.

As incomes have grown, the ratio of money to national income
has increased greatly, as shown in Table 17.

TABLE 17.   THE QUANTITY OF MONEY COMPARED
WITH THE NATIONAL INCOME, 1800–1950

Year	Money (*Millions*)	National Income (*Millions*)	Money as a Fraction of National Income (*D*)	National Income as a Multiple of Money (*V*)	Wholesale Price Index (*1926 = 100*)
1800	$ 38	$ 677	0.056	17.82	101.6
1810	77	915	.084	11.88	107.7
1820	94	876	.107	9.32	76.6
1830	122	975	.125	7.99	65.6
1840	262	1,631	.161	6.23	71.1
1850	389	2,420	.161	6.22	62.3
1860	689	4,311	.160	6.26	60.9
1870	1,373	6,827	.201	4.97	86.7
1880	2,925	7,227	.405	2.48	65.1
1890	5,503	10,701	.514	1.94	56.2
1900	8,865	16,158	.549	1.82	56.1
1910	16,977	33,064	.514	1.95	70.4
1920	39,884	73,393	.543	1.84	154.4
1930	55,228	75,003	.736	1.36	86.4
1940	70,747	81,347	.870	1.15	78.6
1950	178,568	239,170	0.747	1.34	161.5

Source: See Table 15, footnotes 4 and 7, p. 133.

Table 17 presents some important aspects of the relationships
between money, national income, and prices. Real national income
has risen rapidly. The desire to hold money (measured as a fraction of national income) has also grown. The results have been
that the expanding economy has absorbed immense quantities of
money and an increase in prices, which spread over the entire

period (59 per cent in 150 years) may be described as extremely small, has occurred.

Analysis of the trends of prices since 1890 (when the figures for the quantity of money may be considered to be fairly accurate) shows that prices have usually *risen* in any 10-year period during which the quantity of money has increased by more than 60 per cent and that prices have usually *declined* if the money supply rose by less than 60 per cent in a 10-year period.

MONEY, SPENDING, AND PRICES IN THE FUTURE

In an expanding economy, appropriate increases in money and spending will not cause the price level to go up, but will merely keep it horizontal. The "appropriate rate of increase" depends on the following:

1. The rate of increase in the quantity of goods and services to be exchanged (meaning, substantially, the *real* national income)
2. The rate of change (if any) in the demand for money

The second of these factors was shown in Table 17. The column headed "Money as a Fraction of National Income" represents the demand for money—the desire to hold cash.

The table shows that the demand for money rose enormously during the 150-year period. The figures also suggest that the demand for money may have leveled off during the last 20 years. What will it do in the future? One cannot answer this question with confidence. It may resume its rise; it may remain steady; it may decline. Happily for the purposes of monetary management, it is not necessary to know the answer to this question long years in advance, any more than it is necessary to know weeks in advance how cold a given winter day will be in order to provide enough heat to keep a house warm. In either case, it is necessary only to have an adequate mechanism and then to use it as needed.

In order, however, to get a better idea of what constitutes an adequate mechanism for supplying money, it is useful to make an estimate of the amount of money that will be needed in the future. For this long-range estimating purpose, let us assume that the demand for money (as a fraction of national income) has leveled off at 0.70, i.e., that the people of the nation, in the aggregate, will be disposed to hold an amount of money equal to 70 per cent of the dollar national income.

Forecasting the other variable, the growth in the real national income, is not easy. An estimate was presented in Table 4,* and the following figures in Table 18 taken from that table, are calculated in 1954 dollars. They represent, therefore, increases in *real* national income. The figures in the "Money Needed" column are 0.7 of the corresponding national income. That is, the demand for money is assumed to continue at its 1954 level. If the demand for money were to resume its historical rate of rise, the needed amounts of money would be proportionately increased.

TABLE 18.   ESTIMATES OF THE AMOUNT OF MONEY
NEEDED IN SELECTED FUTURE YEARS, 1960–2000
(In 1954 dollars)

YEAR	NATIONAL INCOME (*Billions*)	MONEY NEEDED (*Billions*)
1960	$ 365	$256
1970	500	350
1980	690	483
1990	950	665
2000	1,300	910

Since the actual quantity of money on June 30, 1954 was $209 billion, the estimated increase that will be needed by the end of the century is $701 billion.

A high degree of accuracy, to repeat, cannot be claimed for

* Page 21.

these figures. If, however, they are reasonably accurate, it i
clear that the United States can continue to absorb immens
quantities of additional money without price inflation and, in
deed, must have great increases in the money supply if pric
deflation is not to occur.

The questions of origins of the increase in the quantity o
money in the past and proper management of it in the future wil
be taken up in Chapters 12 and 13.

SUMMARY

The principal conclusions reached in this chapter are these:

1. In an expanding economy like ours, an expanding money
supply will not cause price inflation, provided that the money
supply does not increase too rapidly.

2. If American economic progress is to continue, without defla
tion, large increases in our country's money supply will be necessary in the future. Estimates have been made as to the amounts
that will be needed in the second half of the twentieth century.

CHAPTER 11

Money, Spending, and Production

LET US NOW ANALYZE THE EFFECTS OF THE AMOUNT OF MONEY and the rate of spending on employment and production. This part of the discussion involves a sharp break with the view long held by economic analysts but perhaps represents the opinion of some.

Many analysts have asserted that a country's *real* prosperity was not affected by changes in its supply of money—whether its money supply was large or small. Their argument was that more money would not make a country better off—since money was not the true substance of real income. Since people do not eat or drink money, it was regarded as merely a means to other ends, and its total quantity was believed not to affect real prosperity.

The only effect of a change in the amount of money was held to be a corresponding change in prices. John Stuart Mill stated with exceptional clarity what was long (and indeed still may be) the dominant opinion. Mill wrote:

We are not only called upon to consider what would be the effect of an increase of money, considered by itself . . . Let us rather suppose, therefore, that to every pound or shilling, or penny, in the possession of anyone, another pound, shilling or penny was added. There would be an increased money demand, and consequently an increased money value, or price, for things of all sorts. This increased value would do no good to anyone; would make no difference, except that of having to reckon pounds, shillings, and pence, in higher numbers. It would be an increase of value only as estimated in money, a thing only wanted to buy other things with; and would not enable anyone to buy more of them than before. Prices would have risen in a certain ratio and the value of money would have fallen in the same ratio. It is to be remarked that this ratio would be precisely that in which the quantity of money had been increased.*

Mill's proposition, expressed in the words suggested in Chapter 9,† is this: An increase in the amount of money causes pure price inflation. The truth is that Mill and his followers were wrong; in fact, the amount of money and the rate of spending have a great deal to do with the real prosperity and employment, especially in an expanding economy.

MONEY, SPENDING, AND EMPLOYMENT

The reasoning underlying the classical view was this: If the amount of money is increased, people will have more money and spend it; the increased demand, however, will not result in the production of more goods but will merely cause prices to rise ("pure price inflation"). Is this proposition valid? It depends on whether or not the economy is operating at full speed when the monetary increase occurs. If it is, there will be little or no jump in employment or production, and the result will be mainly a price rise. In this case, the older analysis is substantially correct.

If, however, the monetary increase occurs when a country has a substantial number of jobless workers and production is subnormal, or if it occurs in an expanding economy the increases in spending and demand will result in more unit sales, in higher

---

* J. S. Mill, *Principles of Political Economy* (Ashley ed.; London: Longmans, Green & Co., Ltd., 1926), p. 492.
† Page 110.

production and employment, and possibly some rise in prices ("pure production expansion" or "mixed inflation").

Mill and many other classical economists apparently assumed that full employment always prevailed and that the economy was static. If these assumptions were true, his proposition about money and prices would be valid.

In the real world, however, a major reduction in demand leads both to price declines and to decreased production and decreased employment ("mixed deflation"). Conversely, an increase in demand, if it occurs in a state of less than full employment, will result in more production and perhaps in higher prices.

Since a reduction in the amount of money usually leads to less spending and less demand, and an increase in money to increased spending and more demand, changes in the amount of money are seen to have a real effect on employment, production, and real incomes.

MONEY AND BUSINESS CYCLES

Does it follow from this line of reasoning that changes in the amount of money are the principal initiating causes of the ups and downs of business? Not necessarily. They may be either the initiating causes, or they may put in appearance after the intiating cause; they can become a re-enforcing factor on either the up side or the down side.

It is quite possible that failure of the nation's money supply to increase rapidly enough, beginning in 1928, set the stage for the depression that started in 1929. The stock market crash in 1929 was a contributing factor. Very quickly thereafter, the money supply stopped growing altogether and started to contract. At that time, the reduction in the supply of money joined the vicious circle of contraction as an important adverse influence. Table 19 shows that the supply of money dropped, along with spending and prices, while unemployment rose. The reduction in the quantity of money was both a result and a cause of the business decline.

TABLE 19.   MONEY, NATIONAL INCOME, PRICES,
AND UNEMPLOYMENT, 1929–1933

YEAR	AMOUNT OF MONEY (*Billions*)	NATIONAL INCOME (*Billions*)	WHOLESALE PRICE INDEX	UNEMPLOY-MENT (*Millions*)
1929	$55.8	$87.4	95.3	1.6
1930	55.2	75.0	86.4	4.3
1931	53.7	58.9	73.0	8.0
1932	45.7	41.7	64.8	12.0
1933	42.0	39.6	65.9	12.8

SOURCES: Of money, national income, and prices, see Table 15, footnotes 4, 5, and 7, p. 133; of unemployment, Table 11, p. 89.

After 1929 the serious decline in the money supply intensified the slump. The money supply stopped declining in 1933, but its subsequent failure to increase adequately prolonged the depression. The inadequacy of the money supply was not overcome until the financing of World War II resulted in a rapid and substantial gain in the amount of money.

PRODUCTION AND EMPLOYMENT DURING WORLD WAR II AND THE POSTWAR PERIOD

Future America can be an increasingly wonderful place as the years go by, if we succeed in attaining our full production potential. The performance of the American economy during World War II and afterwards has furnished final proof of the immense productive capacity of the American economic machine. As government spending for war goods soared to undreamed-of heights and government borrowing from banks pushed the quantity of money up to new highs, the output of America's farms and factories shot up to then-unbelievable levels. The story,

devoid of drama, is told simply in the accompanying table of cold
statistics, Table 20.

The story which these figures tell is impressive. In 1939 the
country was in its tenth year of depression. Some recovery had
been made, to be sure, from the depths of 1932–33, but we were
still a long way from full employment and prosperity. Then,
beginning with the "defense program" in 1940, the federal government began to increase its expenditures. When war came,
these were boosted to immense figures. Taxes were also raised
but not nearly as much. Many of the deficit billions came from
bank credit, thus increasing the money supply. Uncle Sam, in
effect, said to American industry, "Produce all the (war) goods
that you can. Don't worry about not being able to find a market
for your output. I will buy all that you can produce."

With this guarantee, with the lid of inadequate demand taken
off American business, management and labor proceeded to pro-

TABLE 20.   KEY FACTORS IN THE ECONOMY OF THE
UNITED STATES, 1939–1948

Part A

	U.S. TREASURY OPERATIONS [a]				
	CASH RECEIPTS (Billions)	CASH PAYMENTS (Billions)	EXCESS OF RECEIPTS (+) OR PAYMENTS (−) (Billions)	AMOUNT OF MONEY [b] (Billions)	NATIONAL INCOME (Billions)
1939	$ 6.6	$ 9.4	$ − 2.9	$ 65.4	$ 72.5
1940	6.9	9.6	− 2.7	70.7	81.3
1941	9.2	14.0	− 4.8	79.4	103.8
1942	15.1	34.5	−19.4	86.1	137.1
1943	25.1	78.9	−53.8	114.8	169.7
1944	47.8	94.0	−46.1	141.6	183.8
1945	50.2	95.2	−45.0	168.0	182.7
1946	43.5	61.7	−18.2	176.2	180.3
1947	43.5	36.9	+ 6.6	169.2	198.7
1948	45.4	36.5	+ 8.9	172.9	223.5

[a] Fiscal year ending June 30.   [b] As of June 30 each year.

Part B

Year	Average Index of Industrial Production (1935–1939 = 100)	Average Index of Wholesale Prices (1926 = 100)	Average Number of Persons Employed (Millions)	Average Number of Persons Unemployed (Millions)
1939	109	77.1	45.8	9.5
1940	125	78.6	47.5	8.1
1941	162	87.3	50.4	5.6
1942	199	98.8	53.8	2.7
1943	239	103.1	54.5	1.1
1944	235	104.0	54.0	.7
1945	203	105.8	52.8	1.0
1946	170	121.1	55.3	2.3
1947	187	152.1	58.0	2.1
1948	192	165.1	59.4	2.1

Sources: Of Treasury figures, Joint Committee on the Economic Report, *Historical and Descriptive Supplement to Economic Indicators* (Washington: U.S. Government Printing Office, 1953), p. 63; of amount of money, national income, and index of wholesale prices, see footnotes to Table 15, p. 133; of index of industrial production, *Federal Reserve Bulletin*, April 1949, p. 415; of numbers employed and unemployed, Table 11, p. 89.

duce such a huge volume of goods that it was called the "miracle of production." The ironic part is that almost as large a productive capacity had been there all during the thirties, but we had not been able to make and deliver the goods because of lack of effective demand.

During the war, a large part of the goods stream naturally consisted of war goods. But when the war was over, the purchasing power which had been generated by wartime borrowing from banks was still there to finance the civilian demand for producer and consumer goods. The result was that the postwar period witnessed the United States enjoying the first peacetime prosperity and full employment in 16 years. Nay, more, the highest level of prosperity in its history! The index of industrial production was 60 per cent higher in 1948 than the predepression peak, reached in 1929; the national income, after adjustment for the change in the level of prices, was also 60 per cent greater.

THE PRINCIPAL ECONOMIC LESSON OF THE WAR
AND POSTWAR PERIODS

The principal economic lesson of the war and the postwar periods is that prosperity and full employment can be stimulated if the money supply is adequate. The new money was mainly created, to be sure, by an expansion of bank credit lent to the government rather than by loans to business, but the effect on business conditions was unmistakable.

This lesson merits the most careful attention. In the first place, the experience demonstrates the importance of the quantity of money to national prosperity. In the second place, it sheds light on other proposed policies and on the analyses which support them. Specifically, it tests the validity of the proposition that the prolongation of the Great Depression was due to harassing political policies and unfavorable legislation. For instance, New Deal laws, such as the Wagner Act and the Securities and Exchange Act, have been mentioned as having retarded business expansion in the late thirties.

The war and postwar periods provided an acid test of this proposition. None of these acts had yet been repealed or modified significantly, and yet prosperity came. Federal regulation of business was not reduced; it was increased, and yet business moved up to record levels. Indeed, wartime regulation of business via the WPB, OPA, ODT, and many other agencies, was almost complete (and admittedly bothersome to business). Nevertheless, business prospered. Nor were taxes reduced. They were increased to an all-time high. And still production, employment, and profits soared.

The explanation of these contradictory conditions is to be found in the monetary factor and in what it generated—market demand.

Government borrowing created new money with which to buy all the war goods which industry could produce; the money then turned up again, as a demand for civilian goods, in the hands of individuals. People had plenty of money and they spent it freely. There was a big demand for goods; as a result, employers hired more employees to produce more goods, and within a fairly short time unemployment disappeared and prosperity prevailed.

There is, in short, no mystery about wartime and postwar prosperity. No occult explanations are needed. The explanation is clear—more monetary life-blood in the economic *corpus* stimulated circulation and brought vigor to the ailing patient.

IMPORTANCE OF MONETARY FACTORS

The analysis presented in the last several chapters emphasized the role played by monetary factors in influencing this nation's prosperity. This analysis makes it clear that cyclical stability and long-run expansion depend partly on how people use their money and partly on how the quantity of money changes—on how the monetary system works in either increasing or decreasing the supply of cash.

From the analysis we learned that the American monetary system in the past has not worked perfectly in these respects. Our inspection of the American monetary system will continue in the next chapter. Before proceeding and inquiring how our monetary system can be improved, it is appropriate to pause and ask a basic question: "How *should* a monetary system perform?"

In the belief that light can be shed on this problem by consideration of a fanciful monetary system, the reader's attention is invited to a consideration of the potato standard.

THE POTATO STANDARD: A PARABLE

In order to avoid both inflation and deflation and to encourage full employment, the monetary system in an expanding economy

hould provide for a long-run increase in the quantity of money,
his increase being slightly faster in times of slump and slightly
lower in times of high-level activity.

The present United States monetary system—the gold standard
–does not make suitable provision for doing these things. In a
lepression men are thrown out of work, and the quantity of
money contracts. An ideal monetary system would encourage the
production of new money at such a moment and would stimulate
an increase in the quantity of money.

The gold standard does this, to be sure, to a certain extent. A
business slump, by lowering the cost of gold mining (while the
price of gold remains unchanged) stimulates production of gold.
Also, unemployed men may take to the hills with simple panning
equipment and pan gold in mountain streams. The unemployed,
however, cannot readily turn to mining gold. Gold mines are
found in comparatively few places in the United States, and these
places are remote from the centers of population.

If some commodity which can be produced everywhere in the
United States were used as the monetary standard, the situation
would be substantially different. *Potatoes* are such a commodity;
they are raised in commercial quantities in every state. So also
are hay and corn, each of which might have some advantages
over potatoes. There is, indeed, much to be said for a triple
standard, consisting of hay, corn, and potatoes.

But let potatoes be taken as the representative, universally
produced commodity. Let the monetary authority establish a
buying price for potatoes. Then the *market* price could not drop
below the *"mint" buying price*. The potato producers would sell
to the public all that people wanted to buy at that price and
sell the remainder to the monetary authority, which would destroy
them since they are perishable. Should the market price rise
above the mint price (which is quite possible, for although the
monetary authority stands ready to buy *unlimited* quantities of
potatoes at a fixed price, it makes no pretense of standing ready

to *sell* any), the public would purchase the entire crop, and none would go to the monetary authority.

There would be, therefore, no instant check on a rise of the market price of potatoes above the mint price. The effect of such a phenomenon, however, would be that there would be no increment in the amount of potato money as long as that condition obtained. Should a general rise of prices occur, carrying with it the price of potatoes, one limiting factor would be the cessation of the supply of potato money. Should such a rise persist, the central bank could bring into play the usual weapons of restraint.

THE POTATO STANDARD IN A DEPRESSION

Conversely, if a depression were to occur, accompanied by falling prices and unemployment, the usual body of potato producers would be augmented from the ranks of those who had lost their regular jobs. These workers would have to accept lower wages than they received in their regular jobs; otherwise, presumably, they would already have been producing potatoes. Nevertheless, some of them could secure jobs and earn some wages.

Furthermore, as the prices of agricultural products declined, some farmers would shift their land from the production of other commodities to potatoes; shifting of land use cannot occur with respect to gold.

Ability of laborers to get jobs raising potatoes if their wages have declined or if they have been discharged would substantially prevent the cumulative decline in consumer income and spending which would otherwise occur. At the same time, the amount of potato money would begin to increase faster than before. The effect of these conditions would prevent a depression from becoming as serious as it can become under the gold standard.

In these respects, the operation of the potato standard would be fundamentally the same as that of the gold standard. When depression comes, more men produce gold; in times of rising prices, fewer men are thus engaged. Unfortunately, the production of gold is excessively localized; there are only eleven states that produce more than 1,000 fine ounces annually and only six (Arizona, California, Colorado, Nevada, South Dakota, and Utah) that produce more than 100,000 ounces. Most of the states produce no gold at all. Hence, in depression, the unemployed and those who have suffered wage-cuts cannot readily turn to mining gold, for there are no gold mines near them. Potatoes, however, produced in all states, offer alternative employment everywhere.

THE POTATO STANDARD AND THE LONG-RUN SITUATION

Not only would the potato standard operate to cause the amount of money to vary in an appropriate countercyclical fashion; the proposed system also would increase the amount of money in the *long run* at a rate that would prevent either a rise or a fall in the commodity price level. If prices fell, both acres and men would shift from producing other commodities to producing potatoes, thereby stepping up the increase in the nation's money supply. If, conversely, prices rose, a shift in the opposite direction would check the production of potatoes and restrict the quantity of money.

It is not to be supposed, of course, that the potato standard would eliminate the usefulness of central bank policy as a regulator of effective demand. It would be useful and entirely compatible with the potato standard. The combination of the two would encourage: 1. cyclical steadiness of effective demand, 2. a long-run increase in money and in effective demand, 3. full employment, and 4. a horizontal commodity price level.

OBJECTIONS TO THE POTATO STANDARD

One objection to the potato standard might be that everyone would raise potatoes, thereby causing inflation. This may be doubted at once, however. Why should anyone who is not already raising potatoes, start to do so? The only possible reason would be the guaranteed price. If this reason seemed to be operating, the cure would be easy—reduce the mint price.

Another objection is that since potato production depends partly on weather conditions, output might vary rather erratically. The criticism is valid.

Another point might be that it might require several months for an increase or decrease in the potato crop to be realized. This argument is also reasonable.

Perhaps the most serious criticism would be that of *waste*. The potatoes would be destroyed, and the product of perhaps a billion man-hours wasted every year. This also is a fair observation. That this criticism also applies to the gold standard is less clearly seen. The gold that is put into the vaults at Fort Knox is not *destroyed*, to be sure. But its incarceration virtually amounts to destruction.

This criticism—wastefulness—is sound. One might ask, "In exchange for this new money, could not the human effort be utilized to produce something useful, instead of potatoes-to-be-destroyed?" Could we not get highways or schoolhouses, instead of potatoes? These are reasonable questions, and they will be taken up in Chapter 13, where a revised monetary system is suggested.

Before discussing a new system, however, let us take a more careful look, in the next chapter, at the present system.

SUMMARY

The principal conclusions reached in this chapter are these:

1. Contrary to long-accepted economic doctrine, the amount of money and the rate of spending have a lot to do with em-

ployment, production, consumption, real incomes, and prosperity.

2. An increase in aggregate demand, under appropriate circumstances, will affect prosperity favorably; a decrease is virtually certain to have an adverse effect.

3. In an expanding economy like ours, full prosperity cannot be maintained without a suitable long-time rate of increase in demand and in the money supply. Unless an adequate, growing monetary demand for goods exists, full production will not exist.

4. In an expanding economy like ours, a reduction in the money supply will produce or prolong a depression.

5. The injection of new money at times of threatened depression—in order to increase the money supply—would be an anti-depression weapon.

6. The way in which a monetary system should perform has been studied by means of the parable of the potato standard.

CHAPTER 12

The American Monetary System

THE ANALYSIS IN THE PRECEDING CHAPTERS WITH RESPECT TO THE influence exerted by spending and the money supply on the price level and on prosperity emphasizes the proposition that these are vital factors in a country's stability and progress.

First, in the United States or in any other expanding economy (which category includes many other nations), there is a *long-run* need for more money. If the quantity of money grows too slowly, the result is a downward trend of prices; if it increases too rapidly, the trend is upward; if it rises at an appropriate rate, the trend of commodity prices is horizontal.

Secondly, the behavior of the money supply affects the *short run*, cyclical fluctuations. If the money supply contracts when business is declining and rises when business is improving, the amplitude of cyclical fluctuations is increased. If, however, the quantity of money were to change in exactly the opposite manner, the business cycle would be reduced. This means that the amount of money should increase rapidly when business is declining and should increase slowly, or actually decline, when business is improving.

In this chapter, the American monetary system will be examined. We shall ask how well the system has performed in these two respects—long-run expansion and counter-cyclical movement. Although the analysis refers to the United States monetary system, the same principles apply to those of many other countries.

THE CREATION AND EXTINCTION OF MONEY

In the examination of the monetary system, attention will necessarily be focused on the sources of creation of new money and, conversely, on the ways in which money is extinguished. The principal sources from which new money comes are these (in order of their importance):

1. Bank credit—an expansion of bank assets
2. Gold—produced domestically or imported
3. Government currency—e.g., the "greenbacks"

Conversely, the following actions reduce the supply of money:

1. A contraction of bank credit
2. Gold exports
3. Extinguishment of government currency

It will be noted that these lists make no mention of *saving* as a factor affecting the amount of money. It is true that an individual person or even a sizable group of persons can increase money holdings by saving and accumulating cash. Their respective accumulations, however, come out of the cash held by other people. If one group has more, others have less. The total amount has not been changed; it has merely been redistributed. The group as a whole (the entire American people) can neither increase the money supply by saving nor reduce it by dis-saving.

LONG-RUN MONETARY PERFORMANCE

From 1800 to 1950 the quantity of money rose irregularly, except for a major decline in the 1930's. It rose too rapidly in each major war but too slowly between wars. It contracted sharply and disastrously after 1929.

That the monetary system was able to keep on producing larger sums of money during most of the peacetime decades was due in large part to several lucky accidents which came along just in time to rescue the gold standard.

Throughout the first half of the nineteenth century, after 1815, the general level of commodity prices was declining. Then, after gold was discovered in California and Australia, annual world gold production multiplied ten times within fifteen years. This

TABLE 21.   WORLD PRODUCTION OF GOLD, 1801–1949

Year	Average Annual Production	
	Ounces	Dollar Value
1801–1810	572,000	$ 11,815,000
1811–1820	368,000	7,606,000
1821–1830	457,000	9,448,000
1831–1840	652,000	13,484,000
1841–1850	1,761,000	36,393,000
1851–1860	6,448,000	133,248,000
1861–1870	6,110,000	126,302,000
1871–1880	5,567,000	115,084,000
1881–1890	5,128,000	106,006,000
1891–1900	10,165,000	210,124,000
1901–1910	16,093,000	378,070,000
1911–1920	20,651,000	426,898,000
1921–1930	18,381,000	379,770,000
1931–1940	31,551,000	1,001,427,000
1941–1949	27,458,000	961,030,000

SOURCES: Selected Annual Reports of the Director of the U.S. Bureau of the Mint (Washington: U.S. Government Printing Office, 1942, 1948, 1951).

mmense increase in gold production stopped the downward price rend; prices started upward in 1850. This upturn, even though urther stimulated in the '60's by Civil War greenbacks, did not ast long, however. For thirty years after 1865 prices were declin- ng. During these decades, as Table 21 shows, world gold produc- ion declined slightly as the richest ore veins in the new gold ields were exhausted.

BRYAN AND BIMETALLISM

The 30-year decline of prices from 1865 to 1896 was the key actor in the emergence of William Jennings Bryan as a candidate or the Presidency in 1896. Bryan was right on one point—the country was suffering from a shortage of money. His solution, lowever—a return to bimetallism—was perhaps not the ideal solu- ion. Nevertheless, the country's money supply certainly had not been increasing rapidly enough during those decades, and *some* olution was needed.

Bryan was almost elected in 1896. He probably would have been elected in 1900, but by then the gold standard had been rescued by a combination of events: 1. the gold discoveries in the Klondike and South Africa and 2. the development of the cyanide precipitation process, which enabled profitable extraction of the yellow metal from low gold-content ores. World gold produc- tion tripled in ten years. In consequence, prices stopped falling and started to rise. This accidental rescue of the gold standard probably defeated Bryan in 1900.

Gold production continued at the new high level for about thirty years. Then the coming of the Great Depression again stimulated production, but the main reason for the three-fold increase in the *dollar value* of gold production in the late thirties was the reduction in the gold content of the dollar, or—what is exactly the same thing—the increase in the official price of gold from $20.67 per ounce to $35.00 an ounce. This not only caused every ounce of gold produced to represent one and two third times as many dollars but also, by greatly increasing the profit ableness of gold mining, stimulated an increase in the number o ounces that were produced.

Beginning with its establishment in 1914, the Federal Reserve System provided a streamlined method for increasing the amoun of bank credit that could be based on the nation's gold reserves This expansive possibility was used immediately in financing World War I and accomplished a large increase in the country' money supply.

BANK CREDIT

In 1929 the country's monetary gold amounted to $4 billion silver money and government currency to about $1 billion, and the total supply of money to $55.8 billion.

In 1950 the figures were: monetary gold stock, $24.2 billion Treasury currency, $4.6 billion; total money supply, $178.6 billion

These figures make it clear that the big source of new money has been neither gold nor government money but *bank credit.*

Bank credit expanded at a fairly satisfactory rate up to 1929 Then it contracted violently, in circumstances that will be described presently. During World War II it expanded immensely

Inasmuch as bank credit has been the principal source of the money supply, the importance of the proper behavior of bank credit is clear.

BANK CREDIT AND THE BUSINESS CYCLE

The banking system has a natural tendency to change the amount of money in exactly the wrong way. When business is improving, both bankers and businessmen are likely to feel more confident. The businessmen, anticipating a larger volume of business, turn to their banks for loans to enable them to expand their

perations. Bankers, taking a favorable view of the business out-
ook, make the loans. Thus the money supply is increased. This
esult is good if business has been substantially depressed. The
ise in the quantity of money and in the volume of spending en-
ourages and permits expansion. The expansion of bank credit
s good, however, only if it is not carried too far. An undue expan-
ion of bank credit will lead to inflation.

Conversely, when business is contracting, both businessmen and
ankers become more cautious. The former curtail their commit-
nents, reduce their inventories, and voluntarily pay off some of
heir bank loans. The bankers, concerned about the safety of
ome of their loans, may put pressure on businessmen-borrowers
o contract their operations and reduce their loans. Let it be em-
hasized that *these actions are merely the things that a prudent
usinessman or banker would feel obliged to do.* They result,
owever, in a contraction of the money supply that intensifies the
ecline and deepens the familiar vicious circle. The situation is
vell described by Professor Allyn Young's phrase—individual
visdom represents collective insanity.

The causal relationship between changes in business and
hanges in the amount of money runs both ways. A decline in
usiness tends to precipitate a drop in bank credit and, therefore,
n the amount of money. A drop in the amount of money (or even
n *insufficient increase*) causes a decline in business. The problem
s how to prevent the drop in the amount of money. This ques-
ion will be taken up presently.

THE MONEY SUPPLY IN FOUR DEPRESSIONS

The American money-supplying system has displayed this tend-
ncy to contract the amount of money in several depressions—
nost violently after 1929. Consider the behavior of the money
upply during the depression of the 1890's. In only one of these
ears, 1893–94, did the quantity of money actually decline—by

TABLE 22.   THE MONEY SUPPLY IN THE
DEPRESSION OF THE 1890'S

Year	Amount of Money (Billions)	Index of Wholesale Prices (1926 = 100)
1892	$5.838	52.2
1893	5.868	53.4
1894	5.787	47.9
1895	6.032	48.8
1896	6.048	46.5
1897	6.205	46.6
1898	7.032	48.5
1899	8.036	52.2

Source: See Table 15, footnotes, p. 133.

1.4 per cent. In all other years from 1890 to 1897, however, the
small increases in money were insufficient to raise the effective
monetary demand for goods to a satisfactory level.

In the Panic of 1907, the money supply behaved as shown in
Table 23. From 1907 to 1908, money dropped 2.6 per cent. The
7.3 per cent increase in the following year, however, shortened
the slump.

TABLE 23.   THE MONEY SUPPLY IN THE PANIC OF 1907

Year	Amount of Money (Billions)	Index of Wholesale Prices (1926 = 100)
1907	$15.102	65.2
1908	14.718	62.9
1909	15.794	67.6

Source: See Table 15, footnotes, p. 133.

From 1920 to 1921, money declined from $39.884 billion to $37.834 billion—5.2 per cent—while the postwar speculative commodity boom collapsed and the price index dropped from 154.4 to 97.6. In another year, however, money had risen to $39.031 billion, and by 1923 to $42.780 billion. The price index was 96.7 in 1922 and 100.6 in 1923.

After 1929, however, the supply of money dropped for four years—a total of 25 per cent—and did not recover to the 1929 level until 1936; then a year later it dropped again. Figures are given in Table 24. Prosperity did not return until 1942.

TABLE 24.   THE MONEY SUPPLY IN THE
GREAT DEPRESSION

YEAR	AMOUNT OF MONEY (*Billions*)	INDEX OF WHOLESALE PRICES (*1926 = 100*)
1929	$55.776	95.3
1930	55.228	86.4
1931	53.685	73.0
1932	45.720	64.8
1933	42.029	65.9
1934	49.000	74.9
1935	53.079	80.0
1936	58.712	80.8
1937	61.527	86.3
1938	60.029	78.6
1939	65.441	77.1
1940	70.747	78.6
1941	79.357	87.3

SOURCES: See Table 15, footnotes 4 and 5, p. 133.

This immense decline in money and the subsequent failure of the money supply to rebound must be regarded as the key factors in the progressive deterioration of the American economy from 1929 to 1932–33 and in the slowness of recovery. Our "growing-boy" economy, which characteristically needs more monetary "life blood" every year, was subjected to a blood-letting that caused the economic body to develop anemia.

Chart 5 shows graphically how much more severe and prolonged was the contraction of the money supply in the Great Depression than in the three previous depressions. In this chart,

CHART 5. THE MONEY SUPPLY IN FOUR DEPRESSIONS

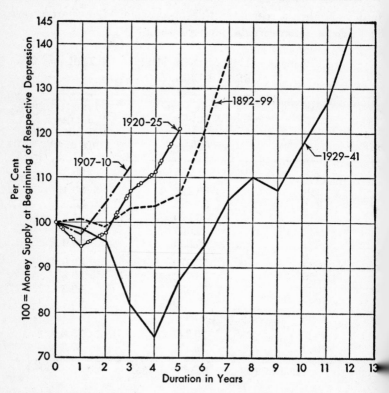

the amount of money in existence at the beginning of each depression is given the value of 100 per cent. Each curve, starting at 100, shows the relative change in the amount of money in the depression to which it pertains.

The performance of the American monetary system after 1929 was so bad that it merits further examination in order to determine why it failed so tragically and what lessons can be learned from the dismal experience.

CAUSES OF THE MONETARY CONTRACTION

The following conditions intensified the contraction in bank credit and the money supply after 1929:

1. Bank failures
2. An outflow of gold
3. A flow of currency out from the banks
4. The passivity of the Federal Reserve System in the face of these compressive forces

The number of bank suspensions had been large from 1921 to 1929, and the deposits of the banks that failed in these nine years totaled $1,623.4 million, as indicated in Table 25 below. In the next four years, however, as banks closed their doors, the loss of purchasing power was unprecedented.

TABLE 25.   DEPOSITS OF SUSPENDED BANKS, 1930–1933

YEAR	DEPOSITS (*Millions*)
1930	$ 837.1
1931	1,690.2
1932	706.2
1933	3,596.7
Total, 4 years	$6,830.2

SOURCE: U.S. Department of Commerce, *Historical Statistics of the United States* (Washington: U.S. Government Printing Office, 1949), p. 274.

The causal relationship between bank failures and the deepening depression was an interacting one. A bank suspension (temporarily at least) extinguishes the amount of money that its depositors have on deposit and thereby reduces their inclination and ability to purchase things. On the other hand, the worse business becomes, the more the solvency of bank borrowers is weakened, and the more the solvency of the banks is undermined. The process again illustrates the vicious circle of economic collapse.

This cruel process could have been ameliorated substantially if the Federal Reserve System had taken appropriate steps to strengthen the position of the banks. The nature of these appropriate steps will be considered after two other pressures on the banks have been noted.

GOLD MOVEMENTS

The pressure on bank reserves was reduced somewhat by the inward movement of gold from 1929 to September, 1931. The United States' monetary gold stock stood at slightly more than $4.0 billion in 1929. A gradual increase took place, carrying the figure up to more than $4.7 billion in September, 1931. Then, presumably as a result of fear engendered by England's departure from the gold standard, a rapid outward movement began. This outflow carried the gold stock down almost to $3.6 billion in the middle of 1932. Thus, between 1929 and mid-1932 the banks' reserves were reduced, net, by $400 million of gold withdrawals. This sizable pressure was in addition to the larger pressure exerted by currency withdrawals.

The gold outflow after September, 1931 came at a particularly critical time and therefore contributed to turning what was already a sizable depression into a near collapse.

FLOW OF CURRENCY OUT FROM BANKS

When the American people want more currency, they typically get it by withdrawing it from their bank accounts. The banks supply the currency by drawing on their own cash reserves. This action reduces their *excess* reserves, i.e., the amount by which their actual reserves exceed their legally required reserves.

The importance of the magnitude of excess cash reserves can hardly be exaggerated. If the excess reserves are high, banks are able to increase their loans and investments; conversely, if they are meager (and perhaps declining), banks are obliged to reduce their credit extension. An increase in hand-to-hand circulation of currency will have a serious restrictive effect if excess reserves are low. The amount of currency outside banks increased substantially after the middle of 1930, as shown in Table 26, with concomitant reduction in the excess cash reserves of the banks.

Once again, the vicious circle was seen. Bank failures caused

TABLE 26. CURRENCY OUTSIDE BANKS, 1930–1934

DATE		AMOUNT OF CURRENCY OUTSIDE BANKS	AMOUNT OF CHANGE	
June 30	Dec. 31		In Six Months' Period	Cumulated Beginning June 30, 1930
		(*Millions*)	(*Millions*)	(*Millions*)
1930		$3,369		
	1930	3,605	+$236	+$ 236
1931		3,651	+ 46	+ 282
	1931	4,470	+ 819	+ 1,101
1932		4,616	+ 146	+ 1,247
	1932	4,669	+ 53	+ 1,300
1933		4,761	+ 92	+ 1,392
	1933	4,782	+ 21	+ 1,413
1934		4,659	− 123	+ 1,290
	1934	4,655	− 4	+ 1,286

SOURCE: Mimeographed table prepared by the Federal Reserve Board, 1951.

people to worry about the safety of their deposits; many withdrew their deposits, i.e., exchanged them for currency; the currency withdrawals squeezed the banks and contributed to the failure of some of them.

As Table 26 shows, the banks were required to supply the people with an additional $1,413 million in currency between June 30, 1930 and December 31, 1933. The seriousness of this pressure on the banks is indicated by the fact that the banks had only meager excess cash reserves on June 30, 1930. Neither on that date nor on any date until late in 1932 (after the Federal Reserve finally began to create new member bank reserves by buying government bonds) did the banks have a comfortable quantity of excess reserves. Table 27 shows the excess reserves held by the Federal Reserve member banks, which held about three quarters of the total of bank deposits.

TABLE 27.   EXCESS RESERVES OF FEDERAL RESERVE
MEMBER BANKS, 1930–1933

DATE		EXCESS RESERVES	FEDERAL RESERVE BANK HOLDINGS OF U.S. GOVERNMENT SECURITIES
June 30	Dec. 31	*(Millions)*	*(Millions)*
1930		$ 6	$ 591
	1930	96	729
1931		73	668
	1931	−33	817
1932		162	1,784
	1932	576	1,855
1933		475	1,998
	1933	859	2,437

SOURCE: Federal Reserve Board, *Banking and Monetary Statistics* (Washington: National Capitol Press, 1943), p. 395.

This table indicates how thin was the margin from which the banks had to supply the large currency withdrawals that occurred as the depression grew worse. The banks were squeezed with two consequences: 1. they had to squeeze their borrowers and 2. many banks failed.

ACTION AND INACTION BY THE FEDERAL RESERVE SYSTEM

In 1928 the Federal Reserve authorities became worried about speculation in the stock market. They began to apply the brakes to bank credit. The rate of increase in the money supply dropped. Presently the stock market tumbled, and the Great Depression began. Mr. Hawtrey was probably not being too critical in saying that the restrictive credit policy stopped speculation by stopping prosperity.*

As business got worse, the pressures (described in the preceding sections) began to appear, forcing a contraction in bank credit and the money supply and thereby intensifying the slump.

What did the Federal Reserve System do in the face of this hurricane? Practically nothing—until 1932. To be sure, the Federal Reserve banks slowly reduced their rediscount rates. This action, however, was too slow and relatively unimportant; it did nothing to supply the member banks with the cash that they needed.

What could the Federal Reserve System have done? Table 27 (above) holds the key to this question. The Federal Reserve could have started acquiring large amounts of United States government securities in 1930. Changes in Federal Reserve holdings of government securities have two important aspects: 1. they comprise the most important action-area where the Federal Reserve can take the initiative and 2. they directly affect member banks' excess reserves.

* R. G. Hawtrey, *The Art of Central Banking* (New York: Longmans, Green & Co., Inc., 1932), p. 77.

When the Federal Reserve banks buy government bonds in the open market, their payments turn up at once in the reserve accounts of the member banks. At any time during the grim months of 1931 the Federal Reserve could have taken the pressure off the member banks by making substantial purchases of government bonds, thereby supplying the member banks with cash. But they did not; the small increases in their holdings during 1930 and 1931, though slightly helpful, were too insignificant to meet the need.

At long last, in 1932, the Reserve banks began to buy fairly large amounts of government bonds in the open market. Payments for these purchases increased the reserves of the member banks. Within a few months the member banks, instead of having to struggle to find the cash to meet demands on them, found that the pressure was off, and they actually had the comfortable experience of seeing their cash reserves rising rapidly above the legally required amounts, i.e., their *excess* reserves increased rapidly. These interrelated figures are shown in Table 27, above.

FEDERAL RESERVE POLICY IN 1936 AND 1937

The Federal Reserve maintained this comfortable situation through 1935 and then took steps to cut the member banks' excess reserves. In 1936 and 1937 the Federal Reserve, utilizing its new authority to change the minimum reserve requirements, *doubled them.* The increase in the *required* reserves reduced the *excess* reserves. Excess reserves amounted to $2.9 billion in July, 1936 but dropped to less than $1.0 billion in May, 1937. The banks, which had been expanding their credit, reversed their policies, contracting their loans and investments by more than $2.3 billion, and the money supply dropped by $1.5 billion. (A net gold inflow of $655 million cushioned the decline in the money supply.) The sharp business recession of 1937 was undoubtedly caused in part by this action of the Federal Reserve.

Fortunately (for the United States, at least), the substantial inward flow of gold, which had begun in 1934, continued. Excess reserves, therefore, began to grow again and in 1938 rose to $2.5 billion. Bank credit expansion was resumed, and business recovered from the mid-depression slump.

In retrospect, it is hard to understand why the Reserve System could have followed so inadequate a course of inaction and of action. Perhaps the best thing to say is that we are all wiser now than we were then. It is doubtful that the Reserve authorities would ever again throttle recovery or fail to respond to the needs of a compressive situation.

THE MONETARY SITUATION DURING AND AFTER WORLD WAR II

During World War II the United States was in the unusual position of witnessing the creation of *more* money than was needed to accommodate the economic needs of the country. The cause was war-financing.

In 1939 the country did not have enough money. In the writer's judgment, the amount in existence at that time—$65.4 billion—was 10 or 20 per cent smaller than the right amount for 1939. As defense—and, later, war—spending rose, one method of financing used by the Federal government caused the amount of money to rise rapidly. The government financed a large part of its budgetary deficit by the sale of notes, certificates, and bonds to the banks. Between 1939 and 1948 American banks' holdings of government securities rose from $23.1 billion to $101.5 billion—an increase of $78.4 billion. This expansion of bank credit to the government was the predominant factor affecting the quantity of money during that period. The total amount of money rose $107.4 billion in that time.

From a strictly *economic* viewpoint, that was too large an increase. The increases in 1940, '41, and '42 contributed to prosperity and the production of full employment, but the subsequent increases generated too large incomes and too much spending, and, as a consequence, price inflation. Wartime government spending and concomitant money creation were controlled, however, not by economic considerations but rather by political and military considerations.

WHAT OF THE FUTURE?

In this chapter we have been analyzing the operation of the American monetary system to determine how well it has performed in two interrelated functions: 1. increasing the amount of money at exactly the rate needed in an expanding economy (the long-run need) and 2. changing the amount of money in a counter-cyclical manner that will contribute to cyclical stability (the short-run need).

By neither criterion can the system be judged to have worked very well. Over the 150-year period, taken as a whole, the system has actually produced too much money. This result, however, is clearly traceable to the occurrence of wars—and especially to World War II. During the 1930's, however, contraction of the money supply contributed to the depth and length of the Great Depression.

In part, the growth of the money supply was caused by several rather unpredictable occurrences that affected the production of gold. May similar developments be expected to take place in the future? If certain spectacular events should occur, gold production might rise high enough to produce, by itself, all the money needed in the future.

Indeed, it is possible that gold might produce *too much* money. Each ton of *sea water* contains a minute amount of gold. Chemists estimate that in all the seas of the earth there are 10,000,000 tons (*tons*, not *pounds*, or *ounces*).* This gold is worth, at our current

* Estimate derived from data given by Edward Wichers, "Gold From Sea Water—A Wild Goose Chase," *Commercial and Financial Chronicle*, September 25, 1952, p. 18.

monetary price of $35 an ounce, $8,400,000,000,000 ($8.4 trillion). It is 380 times as much gold as the United States had in 1954 and 40 times the 1954 money supply.

If a commercially practicable way of separating gold from sea water were discovered the entire world would have to take vigorous steps to prevent being flooded by a gold inflation which would drive prices sky-high.

Is such an occurrence likely? Probably not. Is it impossible? In these days of the wonders of science, the writer is not prepared to say "No." But—and this is the important thing—the mere statement of the possibility brings out the essentially unscientific nature of a monetary system that permits the quantity of money to depend partly on the necessarily irregular advances of science.

EXPANSION OF BANK CREDIT

In Chapter 10 estimates were made of the amounts of money that the United States will need in future decades. The figures were these:

YEAR	AMOUNT OF MONEY NEEDED Billions
1960	$256
1970	350
1980	483
1990	665
2000	910

Gold production may be expected to supply some of these new dollars. In the future, as in the past, however, gold will probably supply only a minor fraction of the new money needed. The major source of new money has been and is bank credit. A key question, therefore, is this: Will the banks expand their loans and investments enough to provide the major part of the needed new money?

The answer to this question depends not only on the ability and willingness of banks to lend and to invest but of borrowers to borrow in future decades. Since these conditions have been reasonably favorable in past decades and seem to be continuing so, we may presume that they will be reasonably satisfactory in the future—especially if the Federal Reserve System assures that its member banks have sufficient excess reserves. If things work out accordingly, the monetary needs of the expanding economy will be adequately served.

In this connection, it may be wise to consider changing the banking laws in a way to permit banks to invest a fraction of their funds in *stocks*—preferred or common. This authority is now being given to insurance companies. Such action would do two things: 1. enlarge the supply of equity capital and 2. allow a further expansion of bank credit.

To be on the safe side, however, a stand-by mechanism would be helpful. This mechanism would not swing into action unless the regular "machine" failed to produce enough money.

CYCLICAL FLUCTUATIONS IN THE MONEY SUPPLY

Inasmuch as expansion of bank credit is the principal source of new money, and since its contraction reduces the money supply, the key question is this one: Can the expansion and contraction of bank credit be controlled in such a way as to minimize cyclical fluctuations in business?

The circumstances that contributed to the catastrophic decline in the money supply after 1929 will probably not be repeated in the foreseeable future. Bank failures are likely to be very few in the future. The banks are stronger; most deposits are now insured; for both of these reasons excessive currency withdrawals are less likely to occur. Moreover, in the unlikely event that such pressures should develop, the Federal Reserve System presumably would provide well-timed, adequate, and effective assistance.

A pathological condition, therefore, is not likely to develop. There does remain, however, the "normal" tendency of bank credit to go up and down. It is the function of the Federal Reserve to try to eliminate these fluctuations. If the Federal Reserve can do so, cyclical monetary stability would be achieved by the use of the traditional mechanisms of central bank control.

Once again, though, it would be the part of the wisdom to have in readiness a supplementary mechanism that could be utilized if the regular apparatus were not performing adequately. Such a mechanism—a functional fiscal-monetary system—is described in the following chapter.

SUMMARY

The principal ideas in this chapter are these:

1. During the period from 1800 to 1950, taken as a whole, the American monetary system, partly as a result of wars, produced enough money for an expanding economy—indeed, more than enough.

2. In the future the monetary system might produce just enough money—or too much or too little.

3. The present monetary system and controls may be adequate to ensure the right rate of increase.

4. In the past the monetary system has changed the quantity of money in a *cycle-intensifying* manner.

5. The worst instance of this behavior occurred after 1929, and its severity was abetted by inaction and mistaken actions of the Federal Reserve System.

6. The Federal Reserve presumably is unlikely to repeat these lapses.

7. The Federal Reserve may be able to go far toward eliminating the normal cycle-intensifying behavior of bank credit.

8. If, however, the long-run need for more money and the short-

run need for *countercyclical* behavior of the money supply cannc
be achieved completely through Federal Reserve action, a sup
plementary or stand-by mechanism designed to provide addi
tional assistance would be helpful.

9. A fiscal-monetary system capable of providing adequat
assistance for both purposes is discussed in the next chapter.

CHAPTER 13

A Functional Fiscal—Monetary System

THE DISCUSSION IN THE THREE PRECEDING CHAPTERS HAS PUT FLESH on the bare bones of the problems, as these were described in Chapter 9. In that chapter it was suggested that the more individuals, businesses, and private organizations can do toward solving these problems, the smaller will be the role of the government.

The long-run problem is that of securing an appropriate expansion of the money flow—national income, demand, and spending. This requires one or more of the following:

1. An increase in the velocity of circulation of money and
2. A decrease in the demand for money *or*
3. An increase in the amount of money

The history of the nation provides little basis for believing that a long-run increase in the velocity of circulation and a reciprocal decrease in the demand for money will occur. The historical trends, indeed, suggest the opposite. Alteration of these trends could come about only as a result of basic psychological changes in people's attitudes toward holding and using money. Perhaps attitudinal shifts will occur spontaneously, or perhaps

private promotional campaigns (for instance, to persuade people
to buy stocks and bonds instead of holding cash) might turn the
trick. However, in the absence of convincing evidence that these
long-time attitudes toward holding and using money will change
or can be changed, one must presume that velocity of circulation
of money is not going to increase and that the demand for money
is not going to decrease.

This reasoning, therefore, leaves only the third alternative—an
increase in the quantity of money—neither too fast nor too slow.
Can the private sectors accomplish this? The term "private
sectors" means the gold producers, bankers, and bank borrowers
(plus the part-private, part-public Federal Reserve System). As
suggested in the previous chapter, it is quite possible that they
may be able to time the increase in the quantity of money properly.

THE PRIVATE SECTORS AND THE BUSINESS CYCLE

Cyclical stability—the short-run problem—requires steadiness in
the increase of the total flow of money, and this requires one or
more of the following:

1. Avoidance of contraction and overexpansion in the velocity
of circulation of money
2. Avoidance of an increase or an undue decrease in the demand for money and
3. Countercyclical expansion in the quantity of money—a faster
rate of expansion in time of slump than in a period of maximum
prosperity

What can the private sectors do to stabilize these three aspects
of the total flow of money?

Let us begin with *consumers*. Some persons would argue that
consumers can do nothing to stabilize the business cycle. This
argument rests on the proposition that consumers' spending depends on consumers' incomes, that consumer spending does not

hange spontaneously but only when consumer income changes. Other analysts, however, suggest that consumer spending does hange spontaneously. There is some truth in each view. Therefore, consumers can help to stabilize business by 1. not going on a buying splurge in time of prosperity (and running up excessive debts) and 2. not slashing their expenditures if business and employment decline.

It is true that these actions would require a large measure of restraint on the part of consumers. If business is declining and workers are being laid off, the newly unemployed have to reduce their buying, and those still employed are likely to hesitate to buy things whose purchase might be postponed.

This reasoning accordingly suggests that consumers can moderate the amplitude of cyclical swings in consumer spending but that it is not reasonable to expect consumers to achieve complete stability in their spending—at least not without approximate stability in their disposable income.

WHAT BUSINESSES CAN DO

The importance of changes in business spending and other business activities is especially great. Although these, like consumer spending, depend partly on business income, they vary spontaneously and substantially from time to time. Since these spontaneous changes in business spending produce a multiple effect, their impact spreads.

Businesses can stabilize their inventories by avoiding over-inventorying in good times and by refusing to slash inventories when business declines.

Businesses can stabilize their purchases of equipment and machinery by following a similarly steady course.

Businesses can stabilize their construction outlays by developing long-range construction programs and budgets, evening out investment in such long-term projects.

Businesses can stimulate and stabilize the demand for the products by means of several activities in the field of marketing These objectives can be accomplished if businesses:

1. Introduce attractive new commodities and improvements in exist ing ones—basing these actions on careful studies of buyers' preference and latent desires

2. Sell more goods by informative advertising and selling efforts

3. Avoid overselling their buyers in good times and overloading buyers with goods and debts

Bankers and bank borrowers can stabilize the money flows an the quantity of money by avoiding both excessive expansion an undue contraction of bank credit.

Some of the actions listed (like those of consumers) will re quire a great deal of restraint. Indeed, a careful businessman c banker who does not want to see his business or bank go brok cannot be expected to avoid contracting his outlays or his loans i time of a slump, unless he is sure that the slump is going to b mild and short, not severe and long.

It is the writer's belief that such assurance can be provided b the operation of a functional fiscal-monetary system. In this sys tem the financial operations of the federal government—ta receipts, outlays, deficits, and surpluses—can be used to stabiliz spending and, if necessary, to generate a countercyclical fluctua tion in the amount of money.

The federal government is in a position to take bolder action than prudence permits to consumers, business men, and bankers The private sectors are in somewhat the same position as the mic in the old story. The mice all agreed that they would be better of if the cat wore a bell, but they quite reasonably asked, "Who i going to bell the cat?"

"Belling the cat of depression" is a risky, and perhaps impos sible, job for one or even several private firms and persons. It i this writer's belief, however, that it is possible and not very risk for the federal government to lend a hand with the bell.

WHAT THE GOVERNMENT CAN DO

The most important thing that the government can do is to create conditions that are favorable to investment and spending. This means keeping taxes down and enacting only wise legislation. Since these were the conditions that prevailed in the 1920's and since the favorable governmental climate created did not prevent the Great Depression, it is clear that something more than favorable governmental policies is essential. We have been examining this "something more," and we have found that it involves the supply and use of money.

The government can contribute to monetary stability through its financial operations. The various ways in which it can play a part are here referred to as a "functional fiscal-monetary system."

The suggested system is already in operation to a considerable extent. The present needs, therefore, are: 1. a wider understanding of the significance of the policies already in effect, 2. a clearer grasp of the interrelationships, and 3. the adoption of a few additional policies which would provide the country with as up-to-date a monetary system as its marvelous production machine.

HOW THE GOVERNMENT AFFECTS SPENDING
AND THE QUANTITY OF MONEY

The fiscal operations of the federal government inevitably influence the state of business and, if properly managed, can usefully supplement other mechanisms and procedures (both public and private) in providing 1. a long-run increase in the quantity of money and spending and 2. short-run stabilization of spending.

The government is itself a spender, and its cash outgo enters, and becomes a part of, the national income. Conversely, its cash receipts come out of the incomes of the public. The difference between its income and outgo—surplus or deficit—is also important.

A deficit is an offset to saving, or a *permitter* of saving. The effect of government surpluses or deficits on the nation's money suppl are also important. The total effects depend on: 1. what the gov ernment does with surplus money and 2. the method by whic the government finances a deficit.

In the following tabulation the effects of a surplus resultin from different uses of the surplus money are shown.

Use of Surplus Money	*Effects on Quantity of Money*
1. Government pays off debt held by non-banking investors	Unchanged
2. Government pays off debt held by banks	Reduced
3. Government literally destroys money	Reduced

The results of a governmental deficit are the opposite.

Methods of Financing the Deficit	*Effects on Quantity of Money Supply*
1. By selling securities to non-banking investors	Unchanged
2. By selling securities to banks	Increased
3. By direct creation of new money	Increased

Let us turn attention to the various ways in which fiscal opera tions affect the quantity of money and the volume of spending.

SHOULD THE BUDGET BE BALANCED?

One line of thought is opposed to utilizing the government fiscal operations for stabilization or monetary purposes. Accord ing to this view, the budget should be balanced every year. Thus when business improves, federal outgo would be increased and/or (since tax revenues rise) tax rates reduced. Conversely, if business declines, outgo would be reduced and/or tax rates raised in order to keep the budget balanced. The actions described in the preceding two sentences, however, would have the effect of *intensifying the business cycle*. The government would make the fluctuations *bigger*, not *smaller*. The proposal that the government's cash budget should be balanced every year must, therefore, be rejected, unless its proponents can devise satisfactory means of stabilizing business.

A second proposal is that the federal budget be balanced, not every year, but rather *over the cycle*. The government would run a surplus in good years and a deficit in poor years, and the sum of the surpluses would equal the sum of the deficits. This arrangement would be cycle-stabilizing, and the extent of the stabilizing influence would depend on the size of the surpluses and the deficits. The bigger they were, the greater would be the countercyclical effect.

A third possibility resembles the second but differs from it in one key respect, namely, the budget would *not* be balanced over the cycle; the sum of the surpluses would *not* equal the sum of the deficits. The unbalance could occur in either direction: 1. a long-run *surplus* or 2. a long-run *deficit*. A long-run *surplus* presumably would be used to pay off the federal debt. To the extent that bank-held debts were paid off, the money supply would be reduced. Conversely, to the extent that a long-run *deficit* was financed by creating money (in either of the ways mentioned above), the quantity of money would be increased. The merit of this third possibility depends, therefore, on the necessary long-run increase in the nation's money supply occurring without the aid of this long-run deficit policy. If the traditional mechanisms—gold and bank credit, as influenced by Federal Reserve policies—should provide an appropriate increase in the amount of money, the federal cash budget should be balanced, or even show a surplus, in the long run. Since the traditional mechanisms (in peace time) probably will not increase the money supply *too rapidly* it is unlikely that a long-run deflationary budget condition would be necessary. If, conversely, the traditional mechanisms should expand the amount of money *too slowly*, a long-run budget deficit would represent a stand-by machine for creating more money.

The amount of additional money that the United States will need between 1954 and 2000 was estimated (in Chapter 10) to be $701 billion. If, despite skillful management, the production of gold and the expansion of bank credit were observed not to be producing enough money as the years passed, the fiscal position could be altered in the direction of smaller surpluses and larger deficits, with the excess of deficits over surpluses financed by created money.

It is impossible to know—years in advance—how the traditional money-supplying mechanism will work over an extended period. Fortunately, however, such advance knowledge is not necessary. If the potential supplementary-money-producing mechanism exists (as it does, even without any legislation or formal adoption), its future use depends on the extent to which its place and power are understood.

CYCLICAL FISCAL POLICY

A countercyclical or stabilizing fiscal mechanism involves these conditions:

1. In good years
   a. Reduction of government spending
   b. Increase of government income
   c. A cash surplus
2. In poor years
   a. Increase in government cash-outgo
   b. Reduction of government receipts
   c. A cash deficit

These fiscal shifts can be administered under three types of arrangements:

1. Automatic policies
2. Formula systems
3. Discretionary operations

The term "automatic policies" refers to the facts that, without any new legislation, federal revenues rise in prosperity and fall in slump, and also that certain federal outlays (for example, contributions to unemployment compensation payments) drop in prosperity and go up in depression. Thus, in good years or in bad years the respective fiscal conditions described above tend to occur automatically. It is possible that these automatic changes (together with other countercyclical policies) would have enough power to ensure achievement of a reasonable stability.

THE ADVANTAGE OF FLEXIBLE TAXES

Many a treatise on public finance contains the proposition that one desirable characteristic of a tax is that its yield should be relatively stable, not fluctuating substantially with the state of business. For example, an excise tax on a necessary commodity (say, *salt*) is likely to yield a steadier revenue than a tax on a luxury item (say, *diamonds*). In line with this reasoning, a government that levies steady-yield taxes will have neither 1. troublesome deficits in poor times nor 2. tempting surpluses in good times.

The reasoning presented in this chapter, however, suggests a completely opposite principle—for the federal government, at least. This opposite principle is that the best taxes are those whose burden rises and falls greatly with the state of business.

With such a flexible tax, if business slumps, the amount of taxes that people then have to pay declines substantially—thus leaving the people with more disposable income (that is, income *after* taxes) than they would have if they had to continue paying the same amount of taxes. Also, if government expenditures remain steady, the government will experience a bigger deficit. In good times, the reverse of these conditions prevails.

Therefore, if governmental financial operations are to be used as a countercyclical mechanism, flexible taxes are seen to be an automatic anticyclical device and preferable to stable taxes.

Judged by this criterion, how good is the federal government's tax system? Rather satisfactory. In fiscal year 1950 (just before the Korean action started), personal- and corporation-income taxe. produced about 70 per cent of the government's revenue. Since the personal-income tax rates are progressive and since corporate income usually fluctuates more than does the general level of busi ness activity, the yield of these taxes is super-responsive to business conditions. Thus, it would seem that the nation (presumably un wittingly) has adopted two important taxes that vary cyclically and that are therefore, anticyclical in their effect. These taxes are "built-in" stabilizers.

It might be worthwhile to examine all federal taxes in the light of this consideration and to eliminate the steady-yield taxes Two further possible steps would be: 1. to hunt for some new flexible taxes and 2. to seek ways of making today's taxes fluctuate even more than they do at present.

CHANGES IN TAX RATES

The term "formula systems" refers to predetermined action that would be taken in response to fluctuations in business. For example, income tax *rates* could be raised when business improve and lowered when it declines.

Changing the schedule of income tax rates has several notabl advantages over increasing and decreasing expenditures, for in stance, by starting and stopping public works.

1. It is quicker; a change in rates can be put into effect in a few weeks.

2. It does not require as much planning.

3. It is uniform over the entire country and does not affect with special force any locality or any industry.

If income tax rates are reduced, the public's *disposable income* —income after taxes—is increased. The expectation is that the public will spend more, the spending being spread over the entire area of goods. Conversely, if income tax rates are raised, disposable income is reduced, with the result that purchases in all lines are likely to decline.

A variation in the schedule of income tax rates is seen, therefore, to be a very powerful additional weapon for fighting the business cycle.

ADMINISTERING VARIABLE TAX RATES

The usefulness of variable tax rates as a countercyclical weapon prompts consideration of the problem of their administration. When would tax rates be changed? How? And by whom?

One possibility would be for the Congress to pass a new law each time the rates should be changed. Since the process of enacting a law is usually rather slow, there would be danger that action would be taken too late.

A second possibility would be for the Congress to authorize the President to change tax rates—perhaps with the advice of the Federal Stabilization Board (described later in this chapter). This arrangement would be similar to the present law with respect to tariff rates, under which the President is authorized to change import duties. Such an arrangement would obviate the necessity of passing a new law each time the rates were to be changed. It would also permit close integration of tax rate changes with other actions taken by the Federal Stabilization Board.

A third possibility would be for the Congress to enact a

schedule of variable rates, with the amount of variations de-
pendent on a statutory rule. A simple way, for example, of providing such statutory changes would be for the amount of each
individual exemption under the personal income tax to depend
on the percentage of unemployment prevalent in the country.
The law might provide a schedule similar to that given in
Table 28.

TABLE 28. SCHEDULE OF EXEMPTIONS

Percentage of Labor Force Unemployed	Value of Each Exemption
1.99 or less	$ 300
2.00–2.99	400
3.00–3.99	500
4.00–4.99	600
5.00–5.99	700
6.00–6.99	800
7.00–7.99	900
8.00–8.99	1,000
9.00–9.99	1,100

Changes in exemptions could be put into effect quickly. Tax
deductions of employees and their take-home pay would be
affected at once. The relative effect would be greater for low-paid
than for high-paid employees. This means that the changes in
take-home pay would be likely to have a large effect on consumer
spending.

The third method of administering tax rate changes would also
obviate the necessity of passing a new law every time the rates
were to be varied. It would also offer a degree of certainty, which
might be reassuring to business men and others—guaranteeing that
fiscal policy was aimed at preventing both boom and bust.

There are, of course, other possible arrangements for administering variable tax rates. Any administrative plan has some difficulties. The important thing is to select the best one, making sure that it is operated as well as possible.

PUBLIC WORKS

The term "discretionary operations" refers, for example, to a reserve "shelf" of plans for public works. Should automatic and formula stabilizers prove inadequate in sustaining a reasonable level of prosperity, additional employment and income would be provided by initiating some of the items on the reserve "shelf" of public works.

Public works can be started fairly promptly if they have been planned in advance. Once started, however, certain types of public works cannot be suspended without violating contracts or risking the loss of what has previously gone into the projects.

The objects of federal expenditure on public works would have to be chosen with care. They should be as nearly noncompetitive with private industry as possible, in order not to discourage private enterprise and private investment. They probably cannot quite equal the Gold Standard in this respect, since it is the Supreme Boondoggle—first the ore is dug out of the ground; then it is refined; then the gold is transported to Fort Knox; finally it is put back into the ground. There are, however, many other noncompetitive items which are admittedly appropriate objects of public expenditure, such as highways, schoolhouses, libraries, parks and recreational facilities, and flood-control projects. These and similar projects do not need to be constructed regularly every year or without interruption. If the "discretionary operations" are planned with great care, construction at intervals should be an entirely satisfactory arrangement. Intelligent scheduling would require that these works be undertaken during slumps and *in advance of requirements*.

ALTERNATIVE METHODS OF CREATING MONEY

The long-run need for more money may be met adequately by the traditional sources—gold and bank credit. If, however, it is not met adequately, a long-run unbalance of the federal cash budget will provide a way of injecting more new money into the money stream. This additional money can be created either by borrowing from banks or by the outright creation of new money Selling securities to the banks is a familiar process, but the "outright creation of new money" calls for some further explanation.

Does it mean "greenbacks"? No, the process could be simpler and, in a sense, more orthodox. The United States Treasury could be authorized to issue a special type of monetary certificate, for deposit only in Federal Reserve banks. The gist of their legend could be something like this: "United States of America—One Hundred Million Dollars—$100,000,000." When the Treasurer deposited one of the certificates, the amount would be credited by the Reserve bank to the government's deposit account, the monetary certificate appearing among the bank's assets. The certificates should be designated as lawful money, eligible to be pledged against the issue of Federal Reserve notes. Any increase in hand-to-hand circulation that would result would be in the familiar form of Federal Reserve notes. This mechanism could be used to finance a long-run Treasury deficit, if it were necessary to step up the money supply.

Which would be the better way of financing an excess of deficits? Should the orthodox one of selling securities to banks be favored or the unorthodox one of direct creation of new money? The former method might provide some check on government spending, as indicated by unwillingness on the part of banks to buy government securities. Also, since it is a "respectable" way of creating money, it is not open to the charge that it is a fiat money system.

The direct creation of new money, however, has advantages.

It avoids increasing the national debt and the interest charges on the debt. Indeed, some of the directly created money could be used to pay off the debt.

Criticisms of directly created money might include the comment that it would be "fiat money," representing a departure from "sound money." These phrases reflect emotional attitudes. The soundest money is that which serves a nation best.

A criticism of greater significance is that if the government had at its disposal this delightful way of financing expenditures—by printing the money—government expenditures would soar to even greater heights. The force of this argument suggests that the other method of financing—borrowing from banks—is better. To be sure, borrowing from banks would involve a long-run rise in the national debt, which is not good. On the other hand, the rise in the debt is harmful mainly because of psychological factors. Moreover, since the debt would presumably grow much more slowly than the national income, its relative size should decline as the years went by.

SHIFTING THE DEBT TO THE BANKS

There is another way in which the government could increase the money supply without creating a long-run deficit situation, without increasing the debt, and without the direct creation of money. This method involves shifting the debt already outstanding from nonbanking holders to banks, a process sometimes called "monetization of the national debt." In 1950, the public (exclusive of government agencies) held $220 billion of government securities. Banks held $96 billion of this amount. Nonbanking investors—insurance companies, other corporations, state and local governments, individuals, and miscellaneous investors—held $124 billion. Skillful management of the debt could shift some of this $124 billion to banks, thus increasing the money supply. The funds newly borrowed from banks would be used to pay off securities held by nonbanking investors. The absolute upper limit of this source of new money is $124 billion. The practical upper limit presumably would be lower than this amount because many of the nonbanking investors would want to retain government securities, regarding them as desirable investments.

PROBLEMS OF MANAGEMENT

Some of the stabilization instruments discussed in this and the preceding chapter are automatic; others operate according to formula; still others require discretionary management.

The more automatic these devices can be made, the better—that is, provided that the automatic arrangements are sound. If they are automatic—on a sound basis—certain advantages follow: 1. People can count on their operation and know, with more or less accuracy, when they will operate, and how. If the stabilization methods are soundly planned, people will realize that their automatic operation will restrain an inflationary boom or, conversely, provide stimulus in a slump. 2. Automatic devices—*good* ones—relieve people's fears that management by men may not be wise.

The formula method lies in between the fully automatic devices and the discretionary ones. Of the formula mechanisms, it may be said that the more definite the formula (provided that it is sound) and the greater the public belief that the formula will be followed, the better, since the closer the formula device will come to moving into the automatic group.

Some discretionary operations still remain. Examples include: 1. most of the operations of the Federal Reserve, 2. the timing of special public works, 3. the timing of special redemptions of the public debt, and 4. shifts of the public debt to the banks. Even these operations could be moved in the direction of being formula changes. Perhaps, indeed, one should say "moved farther in the direction of being formula changes," inasmuch as they already are really formula changes although the formulae are not very well formulated. Federal Reserve operations, for example, are not carried on in a capricious manner, but rather in response to changes in the business situation. The more definitely the money managers can state their rules of action and then follow them (provided that the rules are sound), the better. And, once again, for the same reasons that support the automatic devices.

ORGANIZATION FOR MANAGEMENT

The importance of maintaining stabilized progress demands that the organizational arrangements for managing the monetary instruments should be the very best that the nation can produce.

Management of these credit and fiscal instruments requires close cooperation between the executive and the legislative branches of the government and understanding among government, businesses of all kinds, and the citizenry generally. In order to achieve these goals, the establishment of three groups is suggested:

1. The Federal Stabilization Board
2. The Congressional Stabilization Committee
3. The Federal Stabilization Advisory Committee

The Federal Stabilization Board would consist, perhaps, of nine members appointed by the President with the advice and consent of the Senate. Board members could be appointed for overlapping nine-year terms. Consideration, indeed, might be given to appointing them for life, but they would be subject to compulsory retirement (with retirement pay) at a stated age. This Board would supersede the present Federal Reserve Board.

Every effort should be made to name outstanding men to this Board, since upon them would fall the heavy responsibility of managing the important control mechanisms. Salaries should be adequate; even more important would be the prestige of the

Board. Perhaps the best way of enhancing the Board's prestige would be the naming of outstanding citizens to it. With such a start, other outstanding citizens would be glad to be appointed as Board vacancies occurred.

The Congressional Stabilization Committee would be composed of the chairmen and the ranking minority members of those standing committees of the Senate and of the House whose jurisdiction is related to stabilization policies. This committee would have a liaison function between the Congress and the Board. It would convey Congressional views to the Board and interpret Board policies to the Congress. When necessary, this Committee would sponsor new legislation deemed necessary to improve the stabilization operations.

Without any specific provision, the Congressional Committee would possess an informal veto power over actions of the Board, since the Committee members would influence the tax laws and appropriation bills and could even go as far as to recommend legislation abolishing the Board. In these circumstances, close cooperation between the Board and the Committee would be imperative, and the former would be in no position to be dictatorial.

The Federal Stabilization Advisory Committee would be composed of representatives of the several sectors of the private enterprise system. Among the sectors that might be represented are these: business, labor, agriculture, banking, newspapers, investors, consumers, and the general public. Here also, every effort should be made to appoint outstanding persons to these honorary, occasional-time posts. The functions of the Advisory Committee would be to consult with the Board and with the Congressional Committee and to interpret these bodies and the private enterprise sectors to one another.

The Board, aided by a research and statistical staff, would have as one of its first jobs the establishment of machinery for the continuing collection and analysis of the necessary data, statistical and otherwise, to give intelligent guidance to action. Many of these data represent figures that are already available, to some extent at least. Probably it would be necessary to expand some of the series and to take steps to secure greater accuracy in the figures, or more complete coverage. Only experience and careful analysis could determine finally what information would be necessary. It seems reasonably certain, however, that reliable figures on the following significant factors would be useful:

1. Employment
2. Unemployment
3. Gross national product and its components
4. National income
5. Money
6. Velocity of turnover of money
7. Demand for money
8. Prices
9. Wages
10. Profits
11. Saving
12. Inventories
13. New orders for goods
14. Population

The information yielded by these statistical thermometers would guide the Board in its discretionary actions. The data would also serve the Congressional Committee in its task of continually reviewing the business situation and recommending an appropriate legislative program. Similarly, these figures would be useful to the Advisory Committee.

DETECTION AND DEFLECTION

Control of cyclical fluctuations requires two things: detection and deflection. The preservation of a given condition necessitates no action at all, as long as that condition obtains; action is called for only when there is a departure from that condition. Then the action called for is corrective action designed to re-establish that condition.

To illustrate by a mechanical analogy, let us consider some type of automatic regulator—say a governor on a steam engine. The function of the governor is to keep the speed of the engine constant. Now, in fact, this constant speed is not maintained. What actually happens is that when the engine's speed falls below the norm, the governor admits more steam in order to increase the speed; when the speed rises above the norm, the governor admits less steam in order to decrease the speed. The variations in speed will be slight if the governor is delicate and if the corrective action is prompt and powerful. If the variations in speed are small, the action of the governor will probably be described as *maintaining a constant speed*. Logically, however, the governor is continually *re-establishing a desired speed*. The governor has only three types of action: 1. inaction, 2. speeding up the engine, and 3. slowing down the engine. The governor is not the only variable affecting the speed of the engine. It is the *balancing* variable. If the net effect of the other variables is to reduce the engine's speed below the norm, the governor's action must be opposed to theirs. The governor's action (if any) is always deflective.

So it is with an economic regulator. Given a norm, the task of regulation is counteraction in the event of departure from the norm, thereby achieving reasonable stability.

FORECASTING AND STABILIZATION

A question frequently raised is whether or not the success of a stabilization program depends on having continuously reliable forecasts of future business conditions.

This question may be approached through use of another analogy. Does the success of a temperature-regulating system for a room or a building depend on having continuously reliable forecasts of the outdoor temperature? This question has to be answered in parts. Let us assume it is summertime. Is an accurate forecast of the severity of next winter's weather necessary in order that the system can be prepared to maintain a satisfactory temperature at that time? Assuming that the heating apparatus is powerful enough (an entirely separate matter), the answer is "No"—provided that enough fuel is available.

The "fuel" in a functional fiscal-monetary system consists of governmental outlays, receipts, and creation or destruction of money. All these can be varied to any extent. Therefore, there is adequate "fuel" for the cyclical stabilization mechanism.

Returning to the temperature analogy, let us now suppose that winter has come. Some days are warmer than others, and the outside temperature rises and falls within the day. Can the room now be kept at an even temperature?

The answer to this question depends on: 1. the quickness with which a departure from the norm can be detected and deflection started and 2. the power of the heating (and cooling) mechanisms. If the thermostat is delicate and if the heat comes on quickly and powerfully (and goes off quickly), the temperature of the room will change but little from the norm. If, however, there are substantial *lags* in these reactions, the variations can be large. If the thermostat is sluggish and if the heat comes on and goes off slowly, the temperature will rise far above, and fall far below, the desirable level. In this case, a reliable forecast of the outdoor temperature will be useful because it would permit the control devices to be turned on and off sufficiently in advance of their slow reactions, the desired temperature thus being preserved.

And so it is with cyclical stabilization devices. If detection and deflection are quick and if the deflective machinery is powerful, no forecast of business conditions is necessary. If, however, the opposite is true, an accurate forecast would be helpful, if not essential.

How quickly and how powerfully can the functional fiscal-monetary system operate? The power of the system, since "fuel" is available to any extent, is surely adequate.

How quickly would it operate? Some parts of the system would react almost simultaneously with changes in business and employment. When a slump occurs, tax receipts drop; unemployment compensation payments rise; and the surplus shrinks or changes into a deficit.

Other changes may occur more rapidly or slowly. A drop in the schedule of income tax rates, for example, could (either on a formula or on a discretionary basis) be brought about quickly. The speed of change of Federal Reserve actions is uncertain. In any event, the impact of a Federal Reserve change may not be felt fully for a few months thereafter.

The writer's own view is that the mechanisms for detecting and deflecting operate or can be operated rather swiftly—at any rate quickly enough to make them well worth using even without a business forecast. If this view is correct, it does not follow, of course, that there is no need to try to improve the techniques of business forecasting. Better forecasts would enable the Stabilization Board to do a better job.

PROPER MANAGEMENT

What are the chances that the entire mechanism would be set up and managed well enough for our nation to achieve the two objectives? These are:

1. High-level cyclical stability
2. An expanding economy

The system could fail from either of two types of error:

1. Honest mistakes
2. Improper, e.g., political influences

That these possibilities would exist is unquestionable. But we are entitled to ask two questions, namely:

1. How grave are these dangers?

2. What are the comparative risks involved in using this system (with its possible dangers) as against those involved in not using it?

In order to get at the answer to the first question, let us consider first the forms that mismanagement might take and secondly what the results of mismanagement would be. The principal forms of possible mismanagement would be one of two: 1. providing *too much* monetary stimulus or 2. providing *too little*. Operation of the stabilization program would not involve activities of the kinds which often lend themselves to political temptation. In a general way, the system would affect the economic temperature of the entire nation. It would not deal with giving jobs, letting contracts, doing favors for individuals, or affecting individual businesses, cities, groups, or persons. It would be essentially an impersonal, national mechanism. There would be no "gravy" to ladle out.

Moreover, mismanagement or politically influenced mistakes could not be *hidden*. If the managers blundered, the error would be immediately evident to the entire nation. If *too much* monetary stimulus were given, the result would be a price rise without an increase in (already full) employment. If *too little* stimulus were given, the effects would be falling prices and an increase in unemployment.

These are not actions which can be taken quietly and pass unnoticed, as can appointing one's relatives to public jobs or letting fat contracts to political favorites. Errors in monetary management would be immediately visible to the entire country. Indeed, the operation of the program would be something like that of a heating and cooling system in an office building. If the system isn't operated correctly, the building gets either too hot or too cold, and everybody in the building realizes it. The building engineer cannot conceal his heat-control mistakes.

This fact—that mismanagement would be so frightfully obvious—constitutes a strong safeguard against both types of error.

If an honest mistake were made, it would become apparent very quickly and could be rectified. An error resulting from improper influences would be advertised to the nation just as rapidly.

THE RISK OF NOT USING THIS PROGRAM

And to what dangers will the nation be exposed if these mechanisms are not used? The answer to this question surely is plain and indisputable. If appropriate mechanisms are not used, we may have another major depression at some future date. A future depression would cause our country and the entire world to lurch to the left. It might mean the end of the democratic, free-enterprise system not only in America but in much of the rest of the world.

On the one hand, we have the small danger of mismanagement of a stabilization program; on the other hand, we have the great danger of mass unemployment and social upheaval. Of the two, the latter is both a greater danger and more likely to occur. Therefore, the less risky course is to establish a stabilization program and to make every effort to see that it is carefully set up and skillfully administered. Distrust of the none-too-perfect machinery of democracy in this matter would result in some form of collective, perhaps tyrannical, management of society in the end.

INDUSTRY AND EMPLOYMENT

The American system contemplates that the vast majority of workers will find jobs in *private* industry rather than with the government. Private industry, however, is limited in the number of jobs it can offer. Private industry can afford to hire only enough workers to make the quantity of goods that it can sell.

When industry sells its goods readily, employment is high; when sales slump, employment declines. To be sure, the preceding sentence might have been inverted, since it is true that when employment rises, sales go up also; when, contrariwise, employment falls, sales decrease. The causal interrelationship is subtle and intricate. But the stubborn fact remains that the eyes of industry see sales as the controlling factor, employment as the result. Therefore, a stabilization program will be successful in keeping private industrial employment at a high level only if that program offers industry a continuous, large market for the goods produced by private industry. That is the aim of the program presented in this book. There is perhaps no form of encouragement to business confidence that surpasses a guaranteed large market for industry's goods.

SUMMARY

1. It is quite possible that the private sectors of the nation's economy may be able to provide the long-run increase in the money supply that is appropriate for our expanding economy.

2. If, however, the private sectors are unable to do this, a functional fiscal-monetary system offers a stand-by mechanism with which to supplement their efforts.

3. The private sectors—consumers, investors, businessmen, and bankers—can do much to stabilize the business cycle, but they can hardly be expected to make their best contributions unless they can be reassured that slumps will not be long or severe.

4. This reassurance can be provided by a functional fiscal-monetary system in which the financial operations of the Federal Government provide countercyclical changes in spending and the quantity of money.

5. Proper management of a stabilization program is essential, and an organizational arrangement has been proposed for that purpose.

6. The operation of the stabilization mechanisms should be made as automatic as possible, on a sound basis.

7. Monetary management involves risks, but these are smaller than the danger of a do-nothing program, which would permit another great depression and social upheaval.

CHAPTER 14

An Integrated Program

THE CONTINUING GROWTH OF THE AMERICAN ECONOMY REQUIRES expansion of both supply (productive capacity) and demand. The task of increasing the nation's productive capacity lies chiefly in private hands rather than in the hands of the government. It requires enterprise, innovations, technological progress, good management, better training, and other factors that increase output per man-hour.

These improvements are, for the most part, the job of private enterprise. The economic role of government is to do only those things that are clearly helpful to the effective functioning of the national economy. This proposition also means that the government should refrain from doing things that are not helpful.

Current trends suggest that the nation's productive capacity will be doubled within the next 25 years. This increase will provide the basis for better living. But it also will double the problem of *demand*. In order to have full employment, demand will have to double also and will have to increase at a steady rate—neither too rapidly nor too slowly; above all, it must not decline. The achievement of this condition of stable and expanding demand will require cooperative efforts by both the citizenry and the government.

In the preceding chapters we have noted that the operation of the private banking system, with appropriate support from the Federal Reserve, may be able to increase the country's money supply enough to satisfy the nation's long-run needs. In order to guard against the contingency that the private banking system might be unable to fully achieve this goal, a functional fiscal-monetary system, properly operated, that would provide supplementary capacity for augmenting the efforts of the private banks has been suggested.

The prevention of fluctuations in demand is something to which the private sectors can contribute substantially. We have noted ways in which consumers, investors, business men, and bankers can stabilize their operations.

We have also observed that, when a business decline occurs, willingness of these people to take actions that are both prudent and affirmative depends on their confidence that the decline will be short. A functional fiscal-monetary system, operated properly and widely understood, provides a basis for such confidence. The operation of such a system, therefore, is an appropriate contribution to stability on the part of the government.

SENSIBLE PRICE POLICIES OF BUSINESS

Business managers can help the nation's economy by reducing the prices of goods whenever technological changes or other production improvements reduce the unit cost of the goods. In many cases, failure to reduce prices on such occasions may be depriving the company itself of the gains that would flow from capitalizing on an elastic demand for its products.

The price-reducing policy may be classified as helpful. Its opposite, a price-raising policy, may be fatal to the prosperity program. If, in order to induce people to spend more freely and thus provide a market for more goods, the quantity of money were increased, the desired effect would be nullified if the sellers of the goods were to increase their prices in the same proportion. In that case, the monetary stimulus would not provide more jobs but would spend itself in price inflation.

This undesirable policy is unlikely to be followed very widely by businessmen. They may be slow to reduce prices, but they are also hesitant to raise them. Nevertheless, the danger is worth noting. A sensible price policy represents another way in which the business community can contribute to stability.

SENSIBLE WAGE POLICIES OF UNIONS

The necessity for sensible wage policies is the same as the necessity for sensible price policies. There is, however, one difference. Because of increasing per capita production, *real* wages will rise gradually through the years. Therefore, unless the cost of living were to decline steadily and fairly rapidly (unlikely and undesirable) the normal trend of money wages must be upward. Money wages, in other words, should rise in relation to the cost of living.

Even though wage rates may be expected to increase gradually, they could be pushed up too rapidly, thereby either encouraging inflation or choking off the attainment of high-level employment. An overly rapid advance of wage rates would either cut down severely on profit margins or would lead to the type of undesirable price increases described in the preceding section. On the one hand, employment would be discouraged because employers would not make sufficient profits. On the other, employment would be reduced because of reduced demand due to the high prices of goods. Or, high-level employment could be purchased at the undesirable price of a continuing inflation of prices and incomes.

THE ROLE OF THE GOVERNMENT

In view of the important part to be played by government in encouraging stability, it is appropriate to ask whether this role involves either: 1. a drift toward collectivism or 2. regimentation of the private enterprise system.

Public opinion polls have shown that the people of America are overwhelmingly opposed to collectivism in any form. And, it seems, with good reason. The American private enterprise system is a demonstrated success. It is not perfect, to be sure, but it has given, and continues to give, rise to economic progress, as well as to social and political gains. The philosophy of the private enterprise system does not completely exclude economic activities by the government, but it does insist that when any expansion of governmental activity is proposed, the case for such expansion must be demonstrated clearly. The private enterprise philosophy also suggests that the citizenry should be on the alert lest expansion of government activities lead to a weakening of the private enterprise system or to regimentation of the people.

It is, therefore, important to ask whether the indicated policies represent collectivism or regimentation. The answer is "Neither." These policies do not undertake to tell anyone what he may do or must not do. They do not tell anyone what he must produce or how he must produce it. They do not regulate the use of materials or of labor. They do not regulate specific prices or wages. They do not dictate consumer expenditure or business outlays.

In an over-all sense, to be sure, the policies do (and must, if they are to succeed) aim at influencing the *national aggregates* of some of these things. Some of these aggregates that would be so influenced would be: 1. the total of bank loans, 2. the nation's money supply, and 3. the total of business and consumer expenditures. The achievement of these goals requires that the behavior of individuals and businesses be influenced. But the elements of specific regulation (associated, for example, with wartime controls) are not present.

Perhaps another comparison with a building may clarify the point. An office building needs a heating system and a cooling system. Assuming a temperature ranging from 20 to 100 degrees Fahrenheit, people could not work in a building without both of these systems. The purpose of the systems is not only to make it possible for people to work in the building but also to create the temperature conditions that are most encouraging to doing good work. But these systems do not regulate what work the people do or their methods of work.

So it is with the national monetary system. The purpose is to create conditions favorable to private economic activity—neither too "cold" (deflationary) nor too "hot" (inflationary). The purpose is to provide enough monetary demand to buy the growing aggregate output of goods and services (i.e., to prevent shortages in aggregate demand) and also to prevent the emergence of excessive demand. The system, however, does not undertake to provide a rising demand for *every* product; even in an expanding economy, the demand for many products will decline—for example, those for horses and buggies. Similarly, the system does not aim at expanding employment in *every* industry or at stabilizing the price of *every* commodity. Specific commodities and industries would still have their ups and downs, within a *total* of economic activity that would be growing.

In an expanding economy, some industries will decline, but others will grow at a faster than average rate. National prosperity depends on shifting the productive resources from the declining industries to the fast-growing ones and also on providing employment for an increasing number of workers.

The basic idea of monetary policy is to provide a suitable total demand for the total quantity of goods and services that the private enterprise system can produce, thus maintaining production, employment, wages, profits, and real incomes in the nation as a whole.

This description of the relation of monetary policy to the private enterprise system gives the answer to the other half of the question asked above, "Do these policies represent a drift toward socialism?" The answer is "No." To be sure, it is possible to call *any* expansion of governmental activities "socialistic." According to this view, public schools, highways, and police and fire departments are "socialistic." Labeling all governmental activities "socialistic" and therefore *bad* amounts to embracing the philosophy of anarchism—that there should be no government at all.

The question of the proper role of the government in the management of monetary policy cannot be "settled" by calling a policy "socialistic." The important question is not "Is it socialistic?" It rather is this: "Do the interests of the nation's economy—a private enterprise economy—indicate that government action is desirable?"

GOVERNMENTAL POLICIES TO ENCOURAGE ENTERPRISE AND INVESTMENT

Governmental policies to encourage enterprise and to stabilize investment are an important part of a prosperity program.

Under an individualistic economic system the establishment of law and order marks the beginning of economic progress; then men, freed of the fear, nay, the expectation, of being despoiled of their goods by marauders, are willing to work and to accumulate goods. From that point on, many factors combine to determine a nation's prosperity. Among them, governmental policies with respect to economic matters hold an important place. Tariffs, taxes, subsidies, protection of property, regulation of competition and competitive practices, control of investment processes, laws relating to corporations, labor legislation, consumer protection, and the

rest of the entire congeries of laws, actions, and activities tha
affect business constitute a vital part of the milieu in which peopl
carry on economic activity and condition, to a substantial extent
the nature and volume of that activity.

Each of the topics listed in the preceding paragraph is a fi
subject for extended discussion, none of which can be under
taken in this book. Fortunately for the adequacy of the prosperity
program, the situation with respect to governmental economi
policies, though not ideal, is far from being as bad as some critic
would have us believe. Putting the matter positively, the presen
status of governmental policies is much less of a hindrance to pros
perity than many critics assert it to be.

Unfortunately, this subject is a battleground for political en
thusiasts. The firing from both sides is so sharp that the middle-of
the-roader who is trying to follow the thread of truth is in grav
danger of being the target of both parties. Calm analysis indicate
that the claims of the opposing schools of political thought wit
respect to the "soundness" of either group's policies are exag
gerated. The truth is that both the Old Deal and the New Dea
witnessed a great deal of unemployment. Governmental policie
in 1929, 1930, 1931, and 1932 were probably what most me
would describe as conservative, and, in a conservative way, en
couraging to business enterprise. Nevertheless, to the bewilder
ment of the captains and the kings, as well as of the commor
man, the great slump began under these conservative aus
pices and plunged the nation into the greatest depression in it
history.

In 1933 came new faces, new activities, new programs; cam
also business improvement (which might have come anyway–
the world upturn began in the summer of 1932). Nevertheless
some unemployment persisted. In March, 1933 when the new
group took over, 14 million were unemployed. Seven years later
although the number was lower, there were still 8 million with
out work.

Under one set of policies the depression began; under another it lingered. The trouble was something other than general governmental policies.

OTHER GOVERNMENTAL POLICIES

Sound governmental policies are a necessary condition for full employment, but they are not a sufficient condition. This proposition can perhaps be illustrated by expanding the analogy used above. If one wishes to keep the interior of a building at an even temperature by means of heating and air-conditioning devices, it is essential that the edifice itself be well-constructed and well-insulated. Keeping the temperature in a bamboo building steady (in the temperate zones), even with heating and air-conditioning devices, would be very difficult, perhaps impossible.

That the edifice be well-built is not enough, however. A well-built structure without any heating or cooling apparatus would be very cold in the winter and very hot in the summer. That the building be properly built is a necessary condition to maintaining an even temperature, but it is not a sufficient condition; in addition, there must be devices for offsetting the tendency of the interior temperature to fall in the winter and to rise in the summer. These devices are the simple ones that warm the interior air or cool it.

Similarly, with the economic system, sound governmental policies are essential, but they are not sufficient. In addition, some mechanisms must be employed to restrain the occasional instability of the free enterprise system.

STRENGTHENING THE PRIVATE ENTERPRISE SYSTEM

The mechanisms and policies described in this book comprise an integrated program in which both government and private sectors would contribute to stability and expansion. Since the role of

the government is substantial, it may seem that the program
represents a long step—away from the American free enterprise
system as we have known it in the past—and in the direction of a
government-controlled economy. This is not true, however. The
entire purpose of the program is to keep private enterprise from
collapsing in some great future depression—to keep private enter
prise vigorous by guaranteeing an adequate demand for the
goods and services which private business can produce.

The government's role would not involve regimentation or a
"planned economy." The program would not involve the government's telling anyone in private industry what he may do or what
he may not do. The government would not "plan production"; it
would not control any business operations nor dictate to anybody.

Rather, the program is a gigantic underwriting of the demand
for goods by measures aimed at maintaining the income of the
American people. The people would be completely free to buy
the goods that they wanted and could afford and to reject the
others. Manufacturers and traders would be entirely free to
make, handle, and sell whatever goods they preferred. The program leaves free enterprise free; it undertakes to make that
freedom prosperous by guaranteeing an adequate demand for
goods.

Private enterprise can provide plenty of jobs and make good
profits only when private enterprise can readily sell all the goods
that the workers produce. The program aims at insuring a continuous, big market for the huge stream of goods that the American economy is capable of turning out when it is running at full
speed; private industry would be encouraged and could and
would run at full speed.

The American free enterprise system will not survive if it fails
to provide continuous full employment. Should large-scale unemployment become chronic in the future and be followed by a business slump which carried unemployment up to 20 million or 25

million, some sort of violent change in our politico-economic system would certainly grow out of the people's desperation. What name and what precise form the new system would have are unpredictable. Whatever its name, however, the new system would almost certainly involve less free enterprise and more collective control.

A serious depression would be a condition that would threaten the present American politico-economic system with revolution. Our system is not threatened by foreign ideologies. Revolution could come in America only as a consequence of prolonged and widespread unemployment.

With proper management, however, our present system not only will survive but will create real freedom from want. In circumstances surrounding an adequate prosperity program the American people will enjoy full employment and a steadily rising standard of living. The average family income, *real* income, will be doubled within 40 years. At the same time, the average work week will decline; at some later date it may get down to 30 hours per week, and summer and winter vacations will be available to everyone. New comforts and new luxuries will increasingly become parts of the standard of living of the mass of the people. Our entire population will have enough goods and enough leisure and enough freedom from fear and insecurity to make a beginning on the important job of living the good life. This happy condition is technologically within our grasp. It is not a dream; it is a real potentiality.

Our job is to make the potentiality become actuality. This requires the business and financial system to be operated in a manner that will release the almost limitless possibilities of the technological-production machine. Such operation can be achieved—and *without* totalitarianism or regimentation—but *with* a minimum of governmental action and a maximum of enterprise and freedom.

THE NEED FOR GREATER UNDERSTANDING

One of the greatest contributions that could be made to stabilized expansion is a wider and deeper understanding on the part of the citizenry of the basic relationships between monetary processes and the level of prosperity. The words of the prophet Isaiah, although not uttered in this particular connection, are true, "And wisdom and knowledge shall be the stability of thy times, . . ." (Isaiah 33:6).

Unfortunately, much of the public discussion of these important relationships in recent years has been colored by political partisanship. Many public statements seem to have been prompted less by the desire to make known the truth than by the desire to defend or to attack public policies for political advantage. The spirit of some of these arguments seems to reflect less the theme of Isaiah than to exemplify the Lord's answer to Job, "Who is this that darkeneth counsel by words without knowledge?" (Job 38:2).

Since the success of any stabilization program depends largely on public understanding and acceptance of it, the necessity for understanding is imperative. A notable organization of leading businessmen, set up to study these problems (and others) and to formulate and publicize suggested policies is the Committee for Economic Development. This large group of thoughtful, public-spirited businessmen supports an expert research staff and publishes valuable books and monographs. The Committee has formulated a stabilization program. Readers who are familiar with the Committee's program will recognize the considerable similarity arrived at independently, between that program and the one described in this book.

Serious efforts on the part of the citizenry to understand these matters and to analyze proposed policies are not limited, of course, to the Committee for Economic Development. Other persons, both individually and in groups, are doing much. Such efforts should be expanded.

SUMMARY

The principal ideas in this chapter are these:

1. The achievement of stabilized expansion requires appropriate actions by both the government and the citizenry.

2. A continuous role of the government is to encourage the effective functioning of the private enterprise system.

3. An integrated program of governmental and private policies and actions is capable of producing stable, rising prosperity in future years.

CHAPTER 15

War and Peace

THE GREAT COST OF WAR IS HUMAN SUFFERING. THE KINDS OF SUF-
fering are so well known that there is no need to list them. The
cost in human anguish far outweighs the economic cost, huge
though the latter is. The prevention of war, the achievement of
peace, ranks, therefore, as a greater humanitarian goal than
economic objective.

It is no mean economic objective, however. World War II cost
the United States alone $300 billion in direct expenditures, not
including interest on the public debt and benefits to veterans.
That amount of money would have built a new home for every
family in the United States. The expenditures for national security
programs in the 1952–53 fiscal year aggregated $52.8 billion. This
amount would almost buy a new automobile for every American
family.

In this chapter, the historical causes of war will be discussed,
and a general program of action designed to achieve peace will
be outlined. In the following chapter, the current conflict between
East and West will be analyzed and a program of action
proposed.

CENTRIFUGAL FORCES AND CENTRIPETAL FORCES

The analysis of war and peace may be approached by asking
two key questions, each of which is followed by a supplementary
question. Here are the four questions: 1. What conditions create
disunity and lead to war? These are the *centrifugal* forces—they
ear the whirling globe to pieces. 2. There is then the supplemen-
ary question—What can be done to reduce or eliminate these
centrifugal forces? 3. The second key question is this: What
factors contribute to world unity, toward the preservation of peace
and toward the offsetting of the disruptive forces? These are the
centripetal forces—they bind us together. 4. How can these centripetal forces be strengthened?

This approach, in short, consists of trying to discover the centrifugal forces and means of restraining them and also of identify-
ng the centripetal forces and means of strengthening them. Let us
apply this analysis first to economic factors and deal with the following questions: First, do *economic* factors contribute to disunity and war, and, if so, what can be done to reduce their effects?
And the second question: Are there *economic* forces which contribute to unity and to peace, or could contribute, and if so, how
can their influence be maximized?

Before proceeding with a discussion of these economic factors,
however, let us pause for a moment to remind ourselves of the
vital necessity of making an accurate and reliable analysis of the
centrifugal and centripetal forces. This procedure should yield a
kind of *diagnosis,* the cure of which requires an effective pre-
scription for peace. If the diagnosis is wrong, the treatment is
almost certain to be wrong. If we make a faulty analysis of the
causes of disunity and war, our methods of eliminating them are
likely to be incorrect. If we erroneously endorse proposals because
we believe that they make for unity when in fact they do not, we
are putting our trust in an inadequate solution.

This kind of behavior would be exactly analogous to that which

sought to prevent fires but produced a mistaken explanation of
their cause, together with inadequate methods of fighting fires.
Putting one's faith in such a fire-control program could easily
result in a holocaust.

The preservation of peace and the establishment of world
harmony must be based on a reliable diagnosis of favorable and
unfavorable conditions if we are to develop a program, both pre-
ventive and constructive, that will be a sound one. With the
objective of understanding the importance of accurate analysis,
let us turn our attention to the role played by economic affairs
in world relationships.

HOW SIGNIFICANT ARE THE ECONOMIC CAUSES?

The proposition that economic factors play an important part in
leading to war or in building peace is not, of course, a new one.
It is but one phase of the economic interpretation of history, a
doctrine to which many scholars have subscribed and which,
notably, has been endorsed by many socialist writers.

Doubtless, desires for raw materials, markets, and investment
opportunities have produced some conflicts among countries, certainly among the English, French, and German business interests
prior to 1914. But were these conflicts the real causes of the outbreak of wars?

Is there not more sense in explanations which run in terms of
power politics for its own sake, including the German naval policy,
and in even such little-known personal matters as the humiliation
which Kaiser Wilhelm suffered when a mock cavalry charge
toward him and King Edward VII at Windsor was so realistic that
the Kaiser became frightened and fell off his horse before the
assembled royalty and nobility?

Prior to 1914 a completely opposite economic argument also
enjoyed considerable vogue. This was the proposition that the

nations of the world had become so economically and industrially interdependent, both in terms of raw materials and finished products, that a large scale war was simply impossible. Indeed, even when World War I broke out, many experts unhesitatingly declared that it could not last more than a few months at the most, since Germany's lack of access to materials would force her to agree to make peace. This line of argument—that economic forces are centripetal in character—was shown to be wrong as the weary years of World War I dragged along.

POVERTY AND WAR

It is also argued that nations get into war because of poverty and hard times. These adverse economic conditions are said to produce a willingness on the part of a people—a kind of desperate willingness, perhaps—to go to war as a sort of last resort to improve their miserable status.

Actual facts, however, lend only what might be called mixed support to this proposition. The aggressor nations in World War II were Germany, Italy, and Japan. It is true that the people of Japan were extremely poor, but there were (and are) many even poorer nations, including populous India and huge China. Shall we say that poverty, rather than state religion (including Emperor-worship), was the condition causing the Japanese people to follow their power-hungry leaders? Germany, however, was one of the rich nations with a high level of per capita incomes. Italy was a middle-level country.

The argument that poverty may lead to war does, however, have a more subtle application. Depression and hard times often lead to shifts in governmental leadership. It did, for instance, in our own country in 1932. President Hoover went into office in 1928 with one of the largest Electoral College majorities in our history. Four years later, largely as a result of the depression, he went out

of office after his successor received an even larger majority. All
over the world governments toppled during that period. In some
countries the disgruntled people said it with ballots; in others they
said it with bullets.

Prolonged hard times make it possible—in countries where
democratic processes are not well established—for dictators to
ply their miserable trade and to get into power by making
promises of food and plenty. And since dictators are more likely
to be war-makers than are democratically controlled governments,
depression, in this very special sense of merely helping dictators
into power, frequently contributes to the outbreak of war a few
years later.

INTERNATIONAL TRADE AND CAPITAL OPERATIONS

International trade and international investment operations are
sometimes pictured as a centripetal force—building international
good will and helping to develop friendship among nations. This
line of thought presents a rather rosy picture of personified nations exchanging one another's products to the mutual benefit of
both and the rich ones lending economic support to the poor ones
to the gain of both.

This happy picture, however, must have been painted by people
who had had no first-hand contact with international buying and
selling and international lending and investing. International buying and selling create both the friendships and frictions created by
domestic commerce. Indeed, the frictions are likely to be more
numerous because language barriers may interfere with a true
meeting of the minds. Simple failure to understand one another's
commercial customs may lead to misunderstanding. Finally, when
a buyer believes that he has not received the quality of goods that
he ordered, or when a seller believes that the buyer is trying to
"do" him (the seller) out of his money, how much more acrid are
the feelings likely to be because there is some "scoundrel"

foreigner" involved than would be the case if the other party were a fellow countryman!

Even more productive of friction than buying and selling are international lending and investing. Even regarding our own countrymen we have the adage, "The way to lose a friend is to lend him money." There is wisdom in the saying, domestically and even more internationally. Surely a review of the international loan experiences in Europe and South America in recent decades does not lend much support to the view that, on the whole, loans have increased the friendship among the nations involved.

Now, to summarize with respect to economic factors. Calm analysis and careful consideration of the facts, as distinguished from rationalizations and fanciful beliefs, lend very little support either to the proposition that economic factors cause wars or to the opposite view—that economic factors constitute a valuable unifying agent in contributing to peace. We would, therefore, be making a fantastic mistake if we should seek to cure causes which are unimportant or, alternatively, put our faith in impotent remedies which will not improve the situation.

In order to clarify a phase of the foregoing analysis that might easily be misunderstood, let us consider a question candidly. Is the foregoing reasoning a doctrine of isolationism, and is it opposed to sound proposals for international economic cooperation and collaboration? The answer to both parts of this question is a definite "No." It is not a doctrine of isolationism. International trade is on the whole a good thing and should be encouraged. International lending and investing, if carried on carefully, are also constructive. But neither field of activity offers any special magic to the preservation of peace.

Sound measures for international economic cooperation and collaboration deserve our support, but of them, also, it is unfortunately true that they do not have the power necessary to preserve world peace.

THE REAL CAUSES OF WAR

If, then, war is not the product of economic witchcraft and if peace cannot be preserved by economic wizardy, where can we look for the keys to the problem? What, in short, are the *true* centrifugal forces which are the real causes of war? How may they be reduced or eliminated? What existing or potential centripetal forces may be utilized to bring nations closer together, thus reducing the possibility of conflict?

These are difficult questions, and their answers are matters about which men disagree. The argument of the preceding section is that on the whole economic factors are of relatively little significance either way except for the periodic occurrence of depressions, which tend to lead to the overthrow of governments and the appearance of dictators.

World Wars I and II seem to suggest that these wars were caused by *dictatorship plus megalomania.* A dictator who wants to expand the power of his country and who has control of the means of influencing public opinion and ordering the lives of his subjects can easily lead his country into an aggressive war. If the Kaiser had not been jingoistic, the world would have continued toward disarmament and World War I would have awaited the appearance of another aggressive man and/or group.

The dictatorial ambitions which led to World War II are, in retrospect, astonishingly clear. Mussolini, who very plainly wanted an Italian empire, went about getting it in a perfectly obvious manner. Hitler was even more ambitious. Wanting at least the whole Western world to become subject to Germany, he was completely frank and obvious in his thinking, planning, and actions. Similarly, the Japanese ruling clique made no secret of its belief that Japan was divinely appointed to rule the entire East and perhaps the rest of the world as well.

There was nothing mysterious about these dictators or about their actions. They were power-hungry men who had achieved virtually absolute authority over their own peoples by methods both of terrorism and of persuasive psychology. They were able, partly by leading and partly by forcing, to push their countries into wars which they—and doubtless also their peoples—thought would win them great gains at comparatively small costs.

Moreover, as we can see now with shocking clarity, their intentions and their preparations should have been perfectly obvious. The leaders made no secret of their plans for conquest. They announced quite frankly, even proudly, to their peoples their plans for conquest. They did not, to be sure, ordinarily use the word "conquest." They spoke rather in terms of achieving the place to which their superior national status entitled them, of bringing the blessings of their civilizations to inferior peoples, and, in Japan, even of the economic gains to be derived from the Japanese-sponsored "greater East Asia co-prosperity sphere."

AMERICAN BLINDNESS TO AGGRESSIVE PLANS

The really astounding thing about the entire situation was that we Americans, with few exceptions, did not take these dictators seriously. It was astounding, because on the one hand the dictators were perfectly frank about their plans for conquest, and on the other hand they were building military machines whose existence could not be kept secret. This, then, was the situation in the 1930's—dictators announcing that they were planning on conquest and building the war machines with which to accomplish the conquest. Despite these facts, which now seem so obvious, it appears that relatively few of our countrymen took them seriously. This blindness on our part was so amazing and undoubtedly contributed so much to the ultimate seriousness of the situation that we are compelled to ask why we were so blind and what we could do to prevent such lack of vision in the future.

Our blindness very much resembled that of the Indian chief of legendary fame. The chief was himself so honest that he thought all other men were equally honest. In the end, he paid dearly for his own honesty when scoundrelly white men cheated him out of all that he had. Similarly, we Americans were so peace loving that it was hard to believe that there could be men, even dictators, who were wicked enough to be planning to lead their people in a campaign to enslave their neighbors and, indeed, perhaps the whole world.

The first contribution, therefore, which the United States can make to world peace is to be perfectly realistic about such threats to peace—to be willing to appreciate the fact that there might be dictatorial leaders whose ambitions might be exactly as bad as they themselves admitted.

FOREIGN BLINDNESS TO AMERICAN POWER

A second reason for our unwillingness to accept at face value the plans of conquest of the dictators was that our people apparently believed, not unreasonably, that countries having limited economic and industrial power surely could not be thinking seriously of attacking the United States of America. We Americans knew how big our country was, knew how productive were its fields and factories; we realized how much of our economic production could be turned, if necessary, to producing war materiel. We knew that our war potential was much greater than that of Germany and immensely larger than those of Italy and Japan.

We apparently assumed that the leaders of these other countries also knew these facts. This assumption, however, was a grave error. Perhaps some of these leaders had visited the United States but not many of them. Specifically, neither Hitler nor Mussolini nor Hirohito had ever been in this country. Doubtless at some time each must have read the figures on tons of steel and bushels of wheat which show so clearly the terrific disparity between the production of the United States and that of his own country. But statistics have a way of not sinking in unless they are reinforced by actual personal acquaintance. Key foreign leaders did not understand the economic power of the United States. We did, but we made a great blunder when we thought that they did, too.

This fact suggests a second important contribution which the United States can make—one which is closely related to the first one discussed above. We must cease to view our country's enormous military potential as a real deterrent to foreign aggression—for the simple reason that the foreign aggressors may have no adequate appreciation of this strength.

It is perhaps not an altogether facetious suggestion that any time a would-be foreign aggressor seems to be rattling the sword he should be invited for a state visit to the United States. Let him be taken all over our country, preferably by automobile, so that he will miss none of it as he would if he were on a fast train racing over the rails or on an even faster plane zooming through the sky. Let him be taken from New York City through the industrial workshops of Connecticut and New Jersey, along the Erie Canal, and then via Buffalo, Cleveland, and Detroit, to Chicago, Milwaukee, and the Twin Cities, on to Seattle, and down the Coast. Let him see the automobile factories, the plane factories, the productive farms, and the shipyards. Then bring him back through the new industrial areas of Texas and the South to Washington for the great ceremonial receptions. And mention to him in conversation Los Alamos and the other atomic and hydrogen bomb centers.

Then, perhaps, having seen with his own eyes that which is so gigantic and amazing, fully understandable only with such visible evidence, he might return to his country (which had seemed so big when he left it) with a revised notion about going out to conquer the world, at least as long as that world included the United States of America.

THE UNITED NATIONS

The third contribution which the United States can make to world peace is cooperating with the United Nations, backing and strengthening that world organization.

It may be argued that the United Nations is a weak reed upon which to lean for the maintenance of peace, that the League of Nations was a failure before it, and that the United Nations will be, also. Not only is this a doctrine of despair; it also neglects some very important facts. The first fact is that the United States never became a member of the League of Nations, and therefore the League was deprived of the support and assistance which we could have given it. Today the significance of the membership of the United States of America in the international organization is even greater than it would have been in the '20's and '30's. The United States was economically the most powerful nation even in that period, but the relative position of the United States is even more important today and will continue to be as far into the future as we can now look.

The second fact which the gloomy doctrine neglects is that the League of Nations represented the first effort by mankind to evolve a world forum and it was hardly to be expected that after centuries of nationalism and warfare the first effort would have been completely successful.

The third fact is that thoughtful men now realize that which apparently most of them did not realize, even after World War I, namely, that international aggression is, even in this day when we flatter ourselves on the level of our civilization, a dangerous menace. In other words, men realize today that neither World War I nor World War II was an accident. Men see that these great conflicts grew out of a definite human pattern—one which could be repeated in World War III unless definite steps are taken to prevent it.

The United Nations, backed by our people and all others of

good will, with a wise program vigorously supported, offers a hopeful aid to world peace.

POLITICAL AND ECONOMIC STRENGTH

A fourth contribution which we in the United States can make is that of keeping our own house in order—by keeping strong and healthy our democratic system of government, maintaining respect for the rights of the individual, and keeping our economic system of free enterprise and freedom of opportunity functioning at a high level. Failure to do these things, coinciding either with political incompetence or a prolonged depression, would threaten our well-being, our internal stability, and our influence—economic, military, and psychological—in the world. Our ability to contribute to peace depends, to a very large extent, on improving the American way of life and making it thoroughly admirable.

This program, moreover, would enable us to demonstrate to the world the operation of a democratic, free enterprise system whose success would be a help and inspiration to friends of democracy and free enterprise in other countries, and at the same time, a weapon against those who would undermine this type of system in favor of communist or fascist dictatorships. A collapse of the American system might very well signalize the collapse of democracy and capitalism all over the world, possibly even the start of a world conflict, perhaps along class lines.

SUMMARY

The chief thoughts presented in this chapter may be summarized as follows:

1. A world race is going on—a race between cooperation and catastrophe. Men of good will have only one course—that of supporting world cooperation. Without that, the fragile thing which

we call civilization may disappear from the face of the earth in a final holocaust.

2. With cooperation, mankind may at long last enter upon an era of good and friendly living that will fairly deserve the name of civilization and genuinely fulfill the promise of peace on earth and good will among men.

CHAPTER 16

The World Conflict

THE CONFLICT BETWEEN COMMUNISM AND PRIVATE ENTERPRISE HAS two principal aspects: 1. military and 2. ideological. In both aspects, the comparative economic effectiveness of the two systems is an important factor, although it is not the only important one. Other significant aspects of the conflict include political and social matters, nationalism, propaganda, psychological influences, diplomacy, and international relations.

The ideological struggle for the minds of men bids fair to continue into the indefinite future. It would be arrested, however, and its nature would be changed somewhat, if a full-scale shooting war should develop. The superior industrial strength of the West suggests that such a war would be won by the free countries. This outcome, however, would not mean that thenceforth there would be no more communist activity in other countries. On the contrary, leftist movements emerging from local discontent would continue and perhaps would grow in some countries.

The eventual outcome of the ideological struggle will depend on the comparative merits of the two systems. Let us therefore examine conditions in Soviet Russia, and compare them with those in the leading private enterprise countries.

THE RUSSIAN GOVERNMENT

The government of the Soviet Union is ostensibly democratic. The country has a constitution that reads well. As a matter of well-known fact the government is not a democracy but a dictatorship. It is a police state, and the people do not enjoy civil rights.

Russia is also a propaganda state. The great instruments of mass communication—the means of influencing the knowledge, the thoughts, and the emotions of the people—are in the hands of the state. These include: schools, newspapers, radio, magazines, books, motion pictures, the theater, and even circuses.

In the main, the Russian people know only what their government wants them to know. They are told untruths as well as truths. Conditions in the capitalist countries are commonly misrepresented by the U.S.S.R. as being inferior to those in Soviet Russia. Children and adults are led to believe that they are better off than are the working classes in western countries.

As a result of this massive system of thought control most Russians believe what their government wants them to believe. As a further result, there seems to be little disposition among Russians to revolt against their oppressive government. In any event, it is virtually impossible to organize a revolution in a country where the police-spy system is so universal and where the government controls the military force.

THE STANDARD OF LIVING

With regard to the economic well-being of the Russian people, it is clear that the standard of living of the average worker is low compared to that of workmen in many Western countries.

In terms of real income the Russian people are extremely poor.

They are housed in what could be considered in the United States incredibly crowded conditions. They have plain clothes and few clothing—or other—luxuries. There has occurred, at various times and in certain regions, an actual shortage of foodstuffs.

Even where there has been no shortage, the food of the mass of the Russian people is simple and inexpensive. A representative menu, which is repeated day in and day out, is made up as follows: for breakfast, a cooked cereal called "kasha," brown bread, and tea; for luncheon, a thick soup, "borsch," based on beets and cabbage but including other vegetables also, bread, and tea. Supper is substantially a repetition of the midday meal. Occasional meat and small amounts of butter, sugar, and milk complete the menu.*

Luxuries and conveniences, such as automobiles, radios, telephones, and television sets, which are enjoyed by the masses in the United States, are available to very few persons in Russia.

In summary, real wages are low; real incomes are small; and the standard of living does not compare favorably with that of the United States or with those of other Western countries. (See Tables 5, 6, and 7.)

The cause of poverty in Russia is the low per capita production. Neither agriculture nor industry is very efficient, judged by Western standards. The production of goods is small, and therefore the standard of living of the Russian people is low.

INDUSTRIALIZATION

Some industrialization has occurred; indeed, the rapid building of capital equipment is sometimes offered both in Russia and abroad as an explanation of the comparative shortage of consumers' goods. This explanation, however, does not stand careful

* This information was obtained by the writer while in Soviet Russia in 1933. Reliable reports suggest that there has been little or no menu change since then.

scrutiny. The question is this: Of the Russian workers engaged in the production of capital, many are merely replacing the capital goods—plants, machinery, etc.—currently being worn out. The remaining workers in production are engaged in making additions to capital. (Farm laborers, who constitute a majority of all workers, are producing consumer goods, as do *most urban* workers.) Only about 26 per cent of the total Russian production effort in 1953 went into capital goods.* If half of this, or 13 per cent, represented the replacement of goods, the other half, admittedly a small proportion of all production, is the fraction by which the Russian standard of living could have been raised— provided that there had been no addition to capital goods, that is, accumulation of capital. This tiny fraction is too small to explain the vast difference between the Russian standard of living and that of the West.

WHAT OF THE FUTURE?

The Russian economy is thus seen to be inferior to that of the West, and especially to the American economy. But what of the future? May not Russia, with a series of Five-Year Plans, catch up with the West, including the United States, or even pass it?

Past trends provide a partial answer to this question. The average per capita income has risen fairly rapidly in the United States, while the average Russian's income has shown little or no improvement. The Soviets have not shown any ability, despite their stories about mechanization and improvement, actually to raise the standard of living of the Russian people. And it is no wonder. Progress depends upon the efficiency of the economic system, and the communist system inherently is not as efficient a system as is the private enterprise system.

Progress depends also on technological improvement, and tech-

* Joint Committee on the Economic Report, *Trends in Economic Growth* (Washington: U.S. Government Printing Office, 1955), p. 284.

ological improvement depends on active and free inquiry—upon what is ordinarily called research. At the present time American industry is spending far more money on research than has ever been spent in the past, and this research outlay is continually bearing fruit.

Because the Soviet Union is a police state, *thinking and having new ideas* are dangerous activities. It is dangerous to have ideas in Soviet Russia since there's no knowing when some new idea may turn out to transgress the Party line or may impinge on one or another of one's superiors; therefore, the safe thing to do is to go right along doing the job according to orders and not undertake to introduce changes.

In the United States, however, there are literally millions of places—factories, farms, offices, colleges—where innovations can be developed, tried, and experimented on without getting permission of any commissar; there may be risk of losing one's pocketbook but not one's life or liberty. There are in the United States nearly 5,000,000 farmers and about 6,000,000 business and professional men and corporations, in addition to hundreds of educational institutions and other centers of research and inquiry. And every single one of these men and organizations represents a potential opportunity for something new to be tried. It is out of similar millions of wellsprings that American progress has come in the past and is going to continue to come in the future.

Some progress is to be expected in the Soviet Union as a result of their own efforts and as foreign innovations are copied. But the rate of progress is virtually certain to be much lower than in the United States.

WILL AN ALL-OUT WAR OCCUR?

In view of the much greater industrial strength of the West, it would appear foolish for the communist nations to start an all-out war. The communists, however, may do so if they hold one or the other of the following beliefs:

1. If they underrate Western industrial strength

2. If they think that a surprise attack will reduce Wester industrial and military strength far more than the retaliator attack will lower the communist power.

The first of those opinions clearly would represent lack (knowledge; the second would be dubious—at the very least. Ur less, therefore, the communist leaders were to be misled by sel deception, their self-interest would argue against becoming ir volved in an all-out war. From their own view it would seem t be wiser to continue trying to expand their sphere by the con bination of propaganda, infiltration, subversion, and force tha has already succeeded in some instances.

THE "ALLIES" OF COMMUNISM

Much of the world offers a good opportunity for application o this technique. In many nations there are conditions that ar favorable to communism and unfavorable to the Western politica and economic systems. Let us examine some of these conditions

1. *Poverty*—"stomach communism" it is sometimes called. Thi is a significant condition, but its importance is easily exaggerated Illness and apathy frequently go with poverty; hunger, disease and misery do not always lead to revolution because the peopl(are too apathetic and too weak to revolt.

Among more well-to-do people, on the other hand, communism sometimes makes many converts, as, for example, in France. But, whether they are starving or comfortable, communist propaganda promises them that they will be better off. It is more than a doubt-ful promise, but it has great appeal.

2. *Ignorance*. Many of the earth's inhabitants—possibly more than half—know little or nothing about the world outside their native village or farm region. They are poor, illiterate, and un-educated. They have no newspapers, books, nor radios. If the

lowing terms of communist propaganda misrepresent the
abby life of the Russian masses, these poor peasants are easily
eceived and do not have enough information to realize that
ey are being deceived. Nor do they have any means of dis-
overing the truth. Lying propaganda, therefore, can be very
fective among them.

3. *Land systems.* In many nations most of the land is owned by
ch land-owners, and the bulk of the people work for them, either
employees or as tenant farmers. This system is a kind of eco-
omic feudalism in which the masses are exploited by the land-
rds.

Communist propaganda suggests to the toiling farmers that,
nder communism, the land would be taken from the landlords
nd become the property of all the people. The propaganda in-
icates that the rent (ofttimes a large share of the farm's product)
ing to the landlord would be divided among the workers,
ereby giving them more to eat.

This propaganda "line," it must be admitted, contains a sub-
antial attraction. Programs of land reform, in countries where
ese conditions exist, would lessen the appeal of communism to
rmers.

4. *Inept governments.* Many countries have governments that
e inefficient, corrupt, and/or reactionary. In these nations, the
overnment typically favors the few rather than the many. The
overnment is dominated by a handful of wealthy people who
ay have affiliations with the military. The government may be,
form, a republic; in actual practice, however, it is not a
emocracy, but rather an oligarchy or a plutocracy.

In such a nation, communists can: 1. point to the inept govern-
ent and 2. claim that under communism the government would
e a "people's republic" and would operate honestly, efficiently,
nd in the interests of the common people. The truth of the first
atement may convince the people that the second statement is
so true. Even a doubter might believe that the people could

hardly be worse off than they are under the existing government

We who believe in democracy would have a difficult time in such a nation because the people in such a so-called republic identify their inept government with real democracy and therefore are not impressed with our claims of the superiority of democracy over communism.

5. *Racism.* The peoples of many of the underdeveloped countries see evidences of a feeling of racial superiority on the part of the white men from well-to-do capitalist lands. In some countries certain railway cars have been labeled "For Europeans Only." White men's clubs have excluded natives; civil and criminal rights have differentiated whites from natives; in these and other ways many foreigners have made it clear that they considered the dark or light-skinned natives to be inferior people for whom the white newcomers felt contempt.

These attitudes may not be significant to the masses in poor countries, but they are galling to the natives who are educated, cultured, and well to do. These men become the native leaders and they may embrace nationalism and/or communism in the hope of throwing out the white foreigners.

6. *Colonialism.* Closely related to the foregoing factor is the experience of many underdeveloped regions that are or have been colonies of white powers. The white powers have often exploited the workers and the natural resources of their colonies. The leaders of colonial peoples demand freedom, and may identify capitalism with colonial exploitation.

7. *The use of force.* No country has ever become communist by vote of the people. In every instance, force and violence were the means used by communists to take over governments and nations.

FORCES ON OUR SIDE

The foregoing listing is impressive. Indeed, it may prompt one to wonder whether there are any conditions favoring our side in the ideological struggle. There are, and here they are:

1. A better political system. Democracy—real democracy—is referable to a communist dictatorship. Democracy (based on ood education) provides better government and more freedom.

2. A better economic system. The private enterprise system is a etter system than communism. The better solution for poor counries is to develop progressive private enterprise rather than to go ommunist, as the analyses in this and earlier chapters indicate.

IS COMMUNISM AN ECONOMIC THREAT IN THE UNITED STATES?

The absence in our country of factors favorable to communism neans that communism has no chance at all in the United States unless we should have another great depression. If that should nappen, we might see the emergence of some sort of collectivism, either by orderly or disorderly means. It is probable that the new system would not be called communism because that word nas no sales appeal but rather generates antagonism. The program might be called "American Progressivism." The philosophy of the movement would not be clearly defined, but its central idea would be that the state would somehow provide full employment. Indeed, whatever its name and whatever its central philosophy, it is virtually certain that its motto is predictable. The motto of the movement would be "Jobs for All."

Such an occurrence in the United States would, of course, be he result of the failure of Americans to solve our own problems. It would not be the result of the importation into our country of any foreign ideology. Collectivism as an imported product could not possibly come to the United States. If collectivism should ever come, it would be a purely domestic product—stimulated by the unhappy results of our own stupidity and planned and executed by American demagogues.

A successful program for maintaining high-level prosperity in the United States in the decades ahead would mean that communism would continue to have no chance at all in our country.

FIGHTING THE WORLD MENACE OF COMMUNISM

At the same time that one can be optimistic about the lack of danger of communism in this country and the possibility of maintaining a strong American free enterprise system, it is not possible to be equally optimistic about the outlook for private capitalism in much of the rest of the world. As the discussion in preceding sections has indicated, the "allies" of communism virtually guarantee that communist agitators are certain to make some headway in the years ahead. How much headway they will make is, of course, unpredictable.

We Americans would naturally like to see democracy and free enterprise successful and spreading throughout the world. We would prefer to see communism checked and reduced. A doctrine of assistance to governments that are threatened by Soviet expansion has been adopted. Doubtless this doctrine is wise, but it has two grave dangers. The first danger is that we may find ourselves supporting governments that although genuinely anticommunist, are also antidemocratic—governments which are dictatorial and/or reactionary. Such a result could mean that we would be supporting a reactionary dictatorship under the guise of preventing communist dictatorship; this would be a rather bad bargain.

The second danger is that we might fall into the delusion of regarding Soviet Russia as the only opponent and neglect the other opponent—communist ideology and its allies. If we fell into this delusion, we might be expending our efforts in the wrong direction and, moreover, expending our efforts in ways which would have no bearing at all on the second problem.

The world-wide struggle between democratic capitalism and communism is in reality a war of ideas and propaganda whose goal is possession of the minds of men. Ideas cannot be fought with bullets, and the minds of men cannot be won by force. The spread of communism can be prevented only by other means.

What are these means? Basically, there are two. The first is to
elp to eliminate the conditions that constitute the great allies of
ommunism—poverty, ignorance, land systems, inept govern-
nents, racism, colonialism, and the use of force. The second is to
nake our own system of democracy and free enterprise work,
nd keep on working, so successfully that it in fact is a genuinely
ttractive system to the peoples of less advanced countries.

Removing the allies of communism is not, however, an easy job.
t requires education, economic progress, and the growth of
emocracy. The problem of aiding the economic development
f the less progressive countries was discussed in Chapter 4.
)emocracy depends on education. Education is both a cause and
n effect of political and economic well-being. With the right kind
f education and a reasonable degree of economic well-being,
lemocracy can function successfully.

The job of demonstrating the successful operation of the free
nterprise system is very largely up to our country. The system
as had its highest development here and can go on to even
reater heights in the future. If the American system is improved
nd kept strong, it will furnish an example of the ideals which we
refer. If, on the other hand, it should be weakened, as it would
y continuous, substantial unemployment or (even more) by a
evere depression, the world would slip rapidly in the opposite
irection. A principal contention of this book is that we can keep
his amazing industrial system of ours running at high speed and
roducing an even higher standard of living for our people,
hus providing a world rallying point against communism.

AMERICAN BUSINESS CONDITIONS AND SOVIET POLICY

The expectations entertained by the masters of the Kremlin
ith respect to the outlook for business conditions in our country
eem to play an important part in shaping Soviet policy and ac-
ions. The Russian leaders apparently expect the United States to

experience a major depression at any time. This expectation influences the Russians in two ways.

1. It generates a noncooperative attitude.
2. It generates fear.

Why does it generate fear? This reaction is purely the result
of straight-line Marxist thinking. Marx taught that the depressions
in the capitalist countries would get worse and worse, and that the
capitalist countries would embark on imperialist wars in order to
rescue their faltering economic status. The Russians remember
our depression of the 1930's, and they anticipate that it will be
repeated in the future. A repetition of such a depression would,
they believe, lead to our going to war—against the natural enemy,
Soviet Russia. Hence, the men in the Kremlin regard our prospective depression as constituting a military menace to their
country.

The Russians, moreover, are made uncooperative and stubborn
by the same expectation of an American depression. They see
clearly (what indeed is true) that our influence in world affairs
would drop sharply if we were to have another great depression,
and that the prestige of the free enterprise-democratic system
would likewise slump severely. At the same time, the effectiveness
of communist propaganda all over the world would be greatly increased. An economically floundering America would constitute a
"horrible example" which would lend itself beautifully to the
interests of communist agitators in all countries. For it is true that
the one thing which communism can honestly promise is full employment. There are plenty of jobs in Russia, although the pay is
wretchedly low. The low pay, however, can be concealed or
misrepresented by communist propaganda.

Since the Russians expect an American collapse and reason
correctly that it would play into their hands—by chopping down
our leadership and prestige while theirs grew—they naturally conclude that there is nothing to be gained in cooperating with us.

They reason that the United States has the prestige and leadership today, but that things will be different in a very few years. Then, they believe, the United States will be down, and Russia will be up. Naturally, from their viewpoint, that period would be a better time for them to influence the world. In the meantime, they adopt delaying tactics.

Their Marxist expectation of an American depression to be followed by our launching an anti-Russian war makes it difficult, if not impossible, for the Soviet leaders to place any reliance on our peaceful intentions and declarations.

Consideration of these facts leads to two conclusions that are of great importance in our relations with the U.S.S.R.:

1. As long as the Russians continue to believe that the United States is going to experience a severe depression, they will be unfriendly and uncooperative.

2. If the Russians could be persuaded that we have in fact found out how to prevent depressions in our country in the future, their attitude might change greatly and for the better.

This description of the Russian beliefs re-enforces the proposition whose validity is becoming clearer every day, namely, if we have another big depression, our prestige and leadership in the world will drop or even disappear; conversely, the maintenance of prosperity in our country is necessary in order to enable us to help the world toward peace, prosperity, and democracy. The maintenance of prosperity in the United States is the first requisite for effective American world leadership. An effective prosperity program is therefore of key importance not only to us but to the world.

SUMMARY

These are the main points made in this chapter:

1. The Russian political and economic systems are inferior to those of the Western countries.

2. Communism has several "allies" in many countries.

3. The democratic, private enterprise system also has powerful "allies."

4. An important element in the world conflict is that of improving our political and economic systems and keeping them strong and meritorious.

CHAPTER 17

The Future Outlook

AT NO PREVIOUS TIME IN WORLD HISTORY HAS THE FUTURE HELD, FOR the entire world, two such sharply contrasting possibilities as does the present time. One possibility is dark with menace; the other is bright with promise.

The menacing possibility is that of a global war—one that might even destroy civilization.

The bright possibility is that of peace and prosperity with full employment and rising standards of living and accompanied by gains in the areas of noneconomic values.

THE MENACE OF WAR

Thanks to the invention of the atomic bomb, the hydrogen bomb, and the guided missile, and thanks to the threat of even more terrible weapons in the offing, military power is now capable of effecting destruction on a scale immensely larger than ever before. So terrible indeed is the destructive power of these modern weapons and so unpredictable the chain reactions which they may set off that a future war fought with these weapons may result in the complete or almost complete destruction of the human race. There might be a few survivors living in caves as did their ancestors tens of thousands of years ago, but civilization as we know it would be gone.

The devastating possibilities of a war of science were dramatically summed up in a statement attributed to Albert Einstein—"I don't know what weapons World War III would be fought with, but I do know that World War IV would be fought with *clubs*." Thoughtful people seem to be aware of the menace of modern warfare, and it is to be hoped that this awareness will aid in building a lasting peace.

THE PROMISE OF PROGRESS

People seem to be much less aware, however, of the promise of economic and noneconomic progress to be expected if peace prevails. This theme, therefore, will be examined.

The discussion, and especially the statistical figures, are presented with special reference to the United States. This emphasis does not mean, however, that this country will be the only nation that will enjoy economic progress in the years and decades ahead. The fact is that all countries can advance. It is true that they will not advance at the same rates, either arithmetically or percentage-wise. The countries that now have the higher per capita incomes are likely to register the largest *arithmetic* gains. A country whose average annual per capita income today is $800 may witness a rise to $1,600 in the next half century—an increase of $800, or 100 per cent.

The poorer countries are unlikely to experience so large an *arithmetic* increase but might make an even greater *percentage* gain. Thus, for example, a country with a $200 average personal income figure might accomplish a gain to $600 in the same 50-year period—a rise of $400, or 200 per cent.

What is stated here about prospective progress in the United States may therefore be taken to apply in the main, and with appropriate adjustments, to the nations of northwestern Europe, to Canada, Australia, New Zealand, and, somewhat less precisely, to the middle-income countries.

The rate of future economic advance in the underdeveloped countries is much less predictable. Economic conditions in the poorer countries depend on alteration of many forces, some of which are deeply rooted in centuries-old culture patterns that are not easily altered. That such old culture patterns *can* be changed is demonstrated by the rapid development of Japan during the past century. That they are *not changed easily*, however, is shown by the fact that, with equal exposure to Western agricultural, industrial, and business methods, no other Eastern country changed its economic ways very much during the same period.

THE FUTURE OF THE AMERICAN ECONOMY

Projections presented in this book suggest that the standard of living of the average American family will more than double in the second half of the twentieth century. This will come about as a result of a combination of factors—a continuing efficacy in the training of our labor force, increased skill in management, a very considerable increase in the quantity of capital goods employed in the production of other goods and services, and, perhaps most significant of all, a tremendous technological development.

We are going into the period of fastest technological development ever known in the world. Future historians may indeed label the era into which we are now moving as the "Atomic Age."

Cheap power—"dirt-cheap power"—is on the way. It may come from atomic energy, from solar energy, or from something else, but it is coming and will further revolutionize American industry.

This cheap power cannot be produced merely by substituting atomic fuel for coal or gas under the boilers that provide steam for the turbines that drive the electrical generators. No; really cheap power will await either the development of a completely new method of generating electricity or the invention of a new nonelectrical method of transmitting and using power.

With cheap power will come cheap water for the entire, great, arid West—from processing of the water of the Pacific and piping it to and through the mountains. Cheap water will alter radically the pattern of our agriculture. Moreover, since industry uses more water than does agriculture, the location of industrial plants will also be notably affected. Both developments will further stimulate the growth of the water-deficient West.

THE LONG-RUN TREND OF PRICES

The prospective increase in the productive capacity of the American economic machine means that our national capacity will rise about 40 per cent every ten years and will be quintupled at the end of 50 years.

A very real problem is then presented: Can a market be found for this truly tremendous increase in the quantity of goods and services that we can produce? If a market is not found, deflation will prevail and prices gradually decline. Proper monetary management, however, can prevent deflation and unemployment. There will be some inflationary forces also—1. government policies to support prices and prosperity and 2. the pressures for wage increases.

On balance, it does not seem unreasonable to conclude that these forces would offset each other, leaving the future trend of commodity prices horizontal, *especially if such a price trend were made the objective of public and private policies.* (This conclusion, of course, is based on the assumption that we do not get involved in a large-scale war.)

NEW COMMODITIES

Our future, higher standard of living is going to be characterized by the introduction of an amazing variety of new commodities. Not only will there be a great increase in the total
stream of goods, but also new goods which one can hardly
imagine will be developed.

The difficulty of suggesting the new commodities that are
coming can best be appreciated if "turning our minds back" to the
year 1850, we were to try to forecast the new commodities that
would be introduced by 1950. Who in 1850 would have had
imagination enough to anticipate the development of automobiles,
busses, trucks, airplanes; telephones (including transcontinental
and intercontinental telephony); air conditioning; automatic
washing, dishwashing, and sewing machines; mechanical re-
frigerators and freezers; vacuum cleaners; pop-up toasters; motion pictures with sound and color; radio and color television;
penicillin and the "miracle" drugs; and last but not least, atomic
energy? And this is by no means the end of the list. Indeed, anyone who had ventured to predict all these things surely would
have been classified in 1850 as an impractical daydreamer.

One of the things we can count on with certainty is much better homes. The average family in another 50 years (and to some
extent during the preceding decades) will be able to afford to put
two or three times as much money (and not depreciated money)
into a home as today's average family can. And the average family
will expect to get, and will get, a home that, for attractiveness,
charm, convenience, and for all sorts of unexpected pleasant
aspects of living, will reach beyond the imagination of any of
us today.

The era of personal aircraft is coming. The contraptions may
be helicopters or some other type of machine, but probably not
airplanes of standard design because they require too much space
and too much skill.

Illnesses will be conquered, longevity increased, and mental as well as physical health improved.

These suggestions may seem fanciful, but in fact they are not even very imaginative. One would need the vivid imagination of a Jules Verne or an H. G. Wells to anticipate even a few of the amazing developments of the future.

THE NATIONAL DEBT

Many persons are concerned about the national debt and seem to believe that it threatens our progress. This view may not be put aside glibly with the traditional argument that the domestically held national debt is really no burden because we owe it to ourselves. It is something of a burden because the interest payments require $6 billion a year, and that means $6 billions of taxes. But there is another side to the argument. Most of the debt ($227 billion out of $275 billion) is held by nonfederal entities— individuals, banks, insurance companies, other corporations, and state and local governments. To these holders, the pieces of paper are *assets*, and to them the interest is *income*. A program of reducing the national debt would involve two difficulties: 1. higher taxes, in the beginning (but lower taxes later on) and 2. the need for the holders of the securities to find other investments. Both problems would be serious if the reduction were rapid but could be handled if it were gradual.

It is worth remembering that the British national debt at the end of the Napoleonic War was twice as large as the British national income; nevertheless, Britain experienced in the following decades her greatest economic expansion. The United States' national debt in 1953 ($275 billion) was substantially less than the 1953 national income of $305 billion.

The real solution to the national debt problem will be found in the growth of the national income. If the debt remains at approximately its present amount, the debt will become proportionately smaller—relative to the national income—as the latter rises.

POSSIBLE IMPEDIMENTS TO PROGRESS

As we look at the prospects for the United States we see a bright future of great progress for our people—barring unfortunate developments. What are some of the things that might happen in the decades ahead to hinder this potential progress under the private enterprise system in the United States?

The first of these would be a disastrous war. Such a catastrophe would throw off these forecasts. War would mean inflation, destruction, and death. The extent of these would depend on the length and severity of the struggle.

THE DANGER OF CREEPING COLLECTIVISM

Public opinion polls have repeatedly shown that the American people are overwhelmingly opposed to collectivism in any form and are equally strong in favor of the private enterprise system. And yet there remains the danger that by taking a series of steps, each small and insignificant in itself, the private enterprise system may be weakened to the point where it would cease to be effective—a process of creeping collectivism.

What are some of the ways in which this might happen? One way would be too much government spending and taxing; these would weaken the incentives necessary to the private enterprise system. Federal, state, and local taxes today take about 30 per cent of the national income. That is high for peacetime, except, of course, we're not really at peace. Any substantial reduction in this figure must wait upon happier international conditions or upon growth in the national income, without a corresponding increase in defense expenditures.

A second factor in this process of creeping collectivism would be an excessive development on the part of the citizenry of a "gimme" philosophy and a parallel expansion of the "hand-out state"—processes weakening personal self-reliance and individual initiative.

A third adverse condition would be a development of excessive government regulation (which already has gone far), putting more and more operations of the private enterprise system in a strait jacket until the entire system ceased to be able to function.

A fourth possibility would be improper government competition with private enterprise. Government enterprises having access to the apparently bottomless purse of the taxpayer can easily present improper competition to private enterprise, endangering the latter's functioning and success.

THE DANGER OF A DECLINE IN THE SPIRIT OF ENTERPRISE

The functioning of the American private enterprise system could be seriously injured by a decline in the spirit of progressive enterprise. As indicated in Chapter 5, England's troubles are traceable, in this writer's judgment, to many causes. One of the most important is the decline of the spirit of enterprise which began many decades ago.

Little sign of this occurring in the United States can be seen. There has been, perhaps, in one or two of the older sections of our land some decline in the spirit of enterprise, but even in those sections there is today a resurgence of vigorous progress.

A combination of the conditions listed in the preceding sections could lead to a decline in the efficacy of the private enterprise system. And the insidious thing about any one of them is that the process could go on little by little—here a nibble and there a nibble—none of the steps being significant in itself. Indeed the full impact upon our society probably would not be realized until a time of crisis when suddenly the system, already weakened, would stagger under the impact of dramatic adverse circumstances. At that point, unfortunately, our country would already have gone past what may be called a point of no return. For it is surely too much to expect that the American people of that day would survey the wreckage and say, "Yes, we see what's happened during these past years; we have taken one step after another that weakened the private enterprise system, and now we must reverse all these policies and get back to a vigorous private enterprise system." No, at that point, being past the point of no return, the American people would probably turn to full-blown socialistic policies.

Confidence in our people, however, leads the writer to believe that we can deal adequately with all the problems of today and tomorrow, as our ancestors dealt with theirs. The important thing is that our people should know that the problems exist, since an informed citizenry is likely to be an effective citizenry. The crucial parts of prevention are not to be blind to these dangers, not to become complacent with our situation or with our expanding progress, but to be well aware that just as eternal vigilance is the price of peace, so eternal vigilance is the price both of continued progress and the preservation of our liberties.

MORAL AND SPIRITUAL STRENGTH

Analysis of the conditions of progress and prosperity has indicated that the American people are going to get richer and richer as the decades go by—even as the work week gradually is shortened. This prospect of a life of greater ease makes it appropriate to ask the following question: As the American people get richer, is it likely that they will become weaker in their moral and spiritual life?

This question is of first importance in and of itself. It is important also because of its bearing on economic progress. Serious moral and spiritual weakness would lead to economic stagnation and to national collapse.

Some analysts believe that moral and spiritual deterioration led to the fall of ancient Rome. According to this view, Roman citizens lost their strength as a consequence of luxurious living. The process was not speedy; on the contrary, it required a few centuries. In the end, however—so runs the theory—Rome, much weakened, was conquered by the barbarians. This sort of danger is described beautifully in Goldsmith's words:

"Ill fares the land, to hastening ills a prey,
  Where wealth accumulates, and men decay."

How stands America today in moral and spiritual terms? On the whole, it seems that the nation is in moderately good condition. There are, however, some danger signs. The magnitude of the crime figures and their trend, shown in Table 29, are two such signs.

TABLE 29.   MAJOR CRIMES COMMITTED IN THE
UNITED STATES, 1947–1953

Year	Total Number of Major Crimes
1947	1,665,110
1948	1,686,670
1949	1,763,290
1950	1,790,030
1951	1,882,160
1952	2,036,510
1953	2,159,080

Source: Federal Bureau of Investigation, *Uniform Crime Reports* (Washington: U.S. Government Printing Office, 1948–1954).
Note: The term, major crimes, includes murder, manslaughter, rape, robbery, aggravated assault, burglary, larceny, and auto theft.

Several of the tables presented earlier in this book, picturing American economic progress, may be viewed by Americans with legitimate pleasure. But Table 29 can be viewed not with pleasure or pride, but rather with dismay and shame among our people.

The big figures in Table 29 are disgraceful; moreover, their trend is upward. Indeed, major crimes have increased faster than the population—from 11.6 per thousand in 1947 to 13.5 per thousand in 1953. The record is bad and has been getting worse. A prolonged continuation of this trend would mean the ruin of the nation.

Moral and spiritual strength is vital—primarily for itself and secondarily because it is basic to other aspects of life, including the economic. The importance of preventing a decline in this strength and of stimulating an improvement makes it clear that these tasks are as important as any now confronting the American people in the decades ahead.

THE MENACE OF COMPLACENCY

The economic accomplishments of Americans—both as individuals and as a people—may be accurately described as remarkable. The very magnitude of our accomplishments, however, could easily lead to a widespread sense of self-satisfaction, a feeling that could cause cessation of progress, or even deterioration. If complacency develops in a person, a firm, a university, or a nation, the result is likely to be stagnation, followed by decline.

Complacency may be described as one form of the moral and spiritual weakness referred to in the preceding section. The importance of avoiding this attitude and of encouraging humility and self-examination is clear.

TOWARD GRACIOUS LIVING

If we deal with all our problems—economic and noneconomic—wisely and courageously, economic progress will enable us to travel farther along the road toward a higher goal than economic advance—that of gracious living.

Up to the present, progress in this direction has been hampered because of economic pressures. Grim economic necessity has dominated much of the life pattern of the American people and has given a sober, Puritanical cast to our thinking. Throughout the history of the United States, except in the old South, the American cultural pattern has been influenced to a large extent by the Puritan mores emanating from New England. The Puritan system of thinking was stern and severe, frowning on gaiety and pleasure. By virtue of these very qualities it had survival value in a difficult economic situation. Moreover, it had character-building value. As the Puritan mores spread beyond New England over most of our country, they undoubtedly contributed much to our national development.

The time is now coming, however, when some relaxation of these stern values is in order; this should encourage some highly desirable changes in the direction of charming, friendly, and gracious living in this country. Economic necessity will continue to be a substantial factor, but its *dominant* control is about to be ended. Then the American people will find themselves under so much less economic pressure that the stage will be set for a basic change in our thinking.

Within a very short time, the economic problem—the problem of making ends meet—is going to be solved substantially for the vast majority of our people. We shall have continuous and adequate employment, a gradually shortening workweek, gradually rising incomes, and a steadily improving standard of living. In these circumstances, we shall find that the task of *making a living* will no longer dominate our thinking; instead, we shall be able to give increasing attention to enjoying living.

To the development of a pattern of pleasanter living, the Old South and the Southwest can make important contributions. The Old South can contribute from its culture, and the Southwest can contribute precious qualities derived from its heritage of Spanish culture—charming qualities of friendliness, gaiety, courtesy, absence of nervous strains, and the love of color, music, dancing, and of living itself. These qualities, are not the vigorous and stern qualities which make for industrial progress. No. But they make for gracious living, and that is going to be our opportunity and our need in the decades ahead. With the economic problem solved, the American people can achieve a better balance between work and relaxation in future years.

Our opportunity is to build a nation characterized by less haste and less tension, more friendliness and more fun, less fear and less worry, more courtesy and more kindness, less hoodlumism and less gangsterism, more decency and more civic consciousness, more beauty, wisdom, and goodness. These things are ultimately more important for mankind than economic progress. In any event, economic advance is not necessarily incompatible with them and may contribute to them.

HELP WITH OTHER PROBLEMS

The achievement of stabilized prosperity will have some salutary effects on other related problems. Poverty and unemployment are "parent problems"—they help to create other disagreeable conditions. Some of the evils which they help to create are these:

1. Restriction of output. Labor unions and business concerns, fearing an inadequate market for their goods and services, restrict their productive activities, thereby retarding a rise in the standard of living. Organizations and unions in the various professions and trades try, in different ways, to restrict training for, and entrance into, their respective groups.

2. Dishonesty. When making a living is difficult, people are driven by economic necessity into various types of dishonesty. Laborers, salesmen, business men, professional men, (even bankers), and others practice various little or big dishonesties to help pay for goods and/or services they need or want.

3. Intergroup frictions. When times are hard, or when fear of hard times prevails, intergroup frictions are encouraged. Organizations, fearing competition, keep out members of unfavored groups or handicap them.

Both the reduction of poverty and unemployment and the improvement of business conditions would reduce the economic pressures that contribute to these unfortunate conditions. If business is good and employment opportunities are plentiful, these happy conditions generally being expected to continue, the solution of many ancillary problems will be aided, also.

PEACE AND PROSPERITY

It is a melancholy fact—but one which cannot be neglected—that the period since the end of World War II has been, for many of the nations of the world, a time of fear, fatigue, bickering, and misery. It is only natural that the countries which fought were fatigued. That those which depleted their resources or were devastated had a hard time to get along is equally natural. That bickering—international and domestic—occurred is somewhat harder to understand. Even in the United States, where despite grievous losses our people were enjoying the highest standard of living in our history and in the world, bickering went on against a background of fear of our chances to maintain peace and prosperity in the future.

The international situation, and especially relations with Russia, did not appear favorable. Our country's experience in the Great Depression naturally caused men to wonder whether another great depression might not occur in the not-too-distant future.

In short, the postwar gloom had a genuine basis in the then current conditions and experiences not too long past. Thoughtful men certainly were on sound ground in believing that war and depression would occur again and that poverty would continue unless adequate means could be found to prevent them.

This book is concerned with finding those means. Certain key points that have emerged from the analysis may now be summarized.

The first key point is the important role which has fallen to the United States with respect to these problems. The enormous industrial strength and the huge volume of economic activity in our country have made us the most influential nation in the political and military fields and an important influence in the world's business cycle fluctuations.

We did not seek this powerful role; indeed, many Americans, because of the responsibilities which the position entails, doubtless would prefer that it had never come to us. But it has. The United States has acquired size and power, and we would be serving mankind (including ourselves) poorly if we were to try to evade playing the part in world affairs that goes with such influence and playing it with as much wisdom and courage and humility as we can muster.

BUILDING PEACE

Several ways have been noted in which we can contribute to the maintenance of world peace.

We can study the centripetal and centrifugal forces, trying to strengthen the former and preventing or offsetting the latter. Among the former, the United Nations is important, and we can support it. Since the only real war threat in the foreseeable future is that of the communist powers, we can concentrate on the establishment of satisfactory relations with them. We have observed that the attainment of this goal depends to a large extent on our ability to ensure no more lengthy or severe depressions in our country.

Indeed, the avoidance of major depressions is the cornerstone of our entire future program. A great depression would: 1. injure our strength and leadership, 2. cause Russia to become more intransigent, 3. precipitate a world depression with concomitant political confusion, and 4. encourage communism all over the world.

We want to be a powerful and a peaceful nation, using our power and good will to build world peace and to assist in developing world prosperity. The maintenance of cyclical prosperity in our own country is important to the achievement of these goals.

If American prosperity can be maintained, it appears that—as a result of patient and intelligent efforts on the part of others and ourselves—the world should be able to make real progress toward ensuring peace and toward the development of a world community.

THE MAINTENANCE OF AMERICAN
CYCLICAL PROSPERITY

The analysis presented in this book indicates that major depressions can be prevented in the future by the combined actions of private enterprise and government. One duty of government is to establish and operate a functional fiscal-monetary system.

The need for such a new system results from the economic and financial necessities of our expanding economy. Our nation needs an expanding money supply, properly timed, in order to provide an adequate market for the huge and growing stream of goods which an expanding economy can produce. An appropriate expansion will not cause inflation but rather will prevent deflation and unemployment. Our present monetary system may fail to do these things and might even again reduce the money supply at a time of threatened depression, as it actually did in the 1930's. Therefore, needed changes in our monetary system have been suggested.

The worst depression in our history, two world wars, and two inflations have occurred within the past three and one-half decades. Men would be thoughtless indeed if they did not wonder whether coming decades are going to see a repeat performance of these miserable conditions.

The plain truth is that future decades may see another war, and they will probably witness another depression *unless something adequate is done to prevent such tragedies.* This book is concerned with the things that can be done.

The conclusion is that if men turn their minds and hearts to the solution of these problems, the nations will be able to achieve a world of peace and prosperity.

Index